Aloft in the Gun-Buses

Aloft in the Gun-Buses

The Exploits of the Flyers and Fighters
During the First World War

Tails Up
Edgar C. Middleton

Exploits in the Air
E. W. Walters

LEONAUR

Aloft in the Gun-Buses
The Exploits of the Flyers and Fighters During the First World War
Tails Up
by Edgar C. Middleton
Exploits in the Air
by E. W. Walters

FIRST EDITION IN THIS FORM

First published under the titles
Tails Up
and
Heroic Airmen and Their Exploits (Extract)

Leonaur is an imprint of Oakpast Ltd
Copyright in this form © 2023 Oakpast Ltd

ISBN: 978-1-916535-42-8 (hardcover)
ISBN: 978-1-916535-43-5 (softcover)

http://www.leonaur.com

Contents

To
G. B.

Preface

The development of flying, the work of the pilots and observers, the new, sure shield of the British Empire in the skies, are beyond all comment, and need no explanation. But the doing on't, the story of it, the dauntless courage of it, have made our hearts leap. The daring and the gallantry of it have made the horrors of bloody war almost worth the while. They have put History to shame, and dwarfed even the *Odyssey* of Homer to insignificance. Ill befits a feeble pen to attempt to trace the deeds of their Golden Book. In due humbleness has this volume been compiled.

While writing this brief Preface, I have to offer my grateful thanks to the editors of *Cassell's Magazine, Daily Chronicle, Daily Express, Evening News, Flying, New York Sun,* and *The Star,* for their courtesy in allowing me to make use of certain material which has already appeared in their respective journals; also, to Major-General Ruck, C.B., for his introduction, and Lieutenant-Colonel John Buchan for his foreword.

E. C. M.

London, 1918.

Introduction

By Major-General Ruck, C.B.
(President, Aeronautical Institute of Great Britain)

In this volume Mr. Edgar Middleton brings home in vivid fashion the everyday life of our airmen in the field and on the seas, including realistic descriptions of many of those dramatic incidents which are part and parcel of their existence.

It is well that such stories should be written now they are fresh in our minds and in the heat of the struggle: it will hearten us up. They will also serve as a reference for future writers in more peaceful times, when it may be possible to analyse the conditions which have given rise to so great a devotion, so complete a triumph of soul over body.

There is no place here for individual praise—a personal compliment would be almost an insult; but I may perhaps be allowed to add my warmest appreciation of the humanity, the dislike of notoriety, and the light-heartedness which punctuate these records.

This war is but the prelude to still greater developments in our social history. Is it not to be hoped that the qualities shown by our gallant airmen, their courage, chivalry, self-denial, enterprise, and buoyancy, will find adequate expression in the new order of things to which we have to adjust ourselves?

As regards the military value of these deeds of skill and self-sacrifice, it is obvious to all and is of vital importance. If our Flying Services had either failed or had fallen short of the high standard they have reached, our present position would have been a most precarious one; whereas now it is generally acknowledged that the overwhelming. superiority in the air which, with the assistance of our Allies, we have every reason to expect in the near future, will lead, ultimately, to the complete success of our cause.

All honour, therefore, to those who have done so much to make such a position possible, and I trust that before the account is closed some recognition may be given to those earlier pioneers in aviation, or to their memories, who, in spite of every discouragement and much ridicule, held to their opinions, carried out the preliminary investigations and trials (many gave their lives also), and laid the foundation for the splendid work of our Flying Service.

R. M. Ruck,
Major-General.

May 25th, 1918.

Foreword

By Colonel John Buchan
(Director, British Ministry of Information)

I am glad that Mr. Edgar Middleton has put together another collection of his admirable aircraft sketches. He knows what he is writing about, he has himself served in the Air Forces, and he has a sense of drama and the picturesque which can do justice to the amazing romance of the aeroplane in war. Modern science has depressed the human factor in other arms, and soldiering today is in the main a matter of masses and the machine. But the same cause has in the Flying Service worked an opposite result. There the possession of one kind of machine takes a man out of the grip of the machine and sets him adventuring in a free world as in the old days of war. No individual exploits of earlier campaigns have ever excelled those of the heroes of our Air Service. The incredible has become the normal, and Tertullian's paradox is sober truth: *Est impossible? Certum est.*

J.B.

CHAPTER 1

Tradition

"Good stories," said an airman friend of mine, recently home on leave from a hard spell of flying over the lines—"to tell the truth, I know very few. At least, there's one or two stunts that—that fellows in our squadron have put up," he sheepishly apologised.

He was in dread terror lest I should ask him any personal reminiscences. Yet, to my knowledge, he had brought down fully half a score of Huns, had narrowly escaped death in a flaming aeroplane, and had been badly winged by Hun "Archies." He was willing enough to talk of others, but of himself—not a word.

Thus, unknowingly, he plumbed the spirit that prevails through every rank of our Flying Service. The air of nonchalance with which the most daring raids are accomplished, to those unacquainted with the British temperament, would savour unfavourably of "swank" and bravado. Yet it is genuine enough, for it has been developed in every schoolboy sports-field in the country—that spirit of "doing one's bit to the best of one's ability, and keeping one's mouth shut very close about it."

Before he took his leave, however, I managed to draw him out sufficiently to tell me of one cool pilot of the R.F.C., who, by every theory of logic, should be wearing a "brass-hat" and directing an army corps. This enterprising youngster—who, by the way, spoke German fluently—landed one dark night beside a German aerodrome. Leaving his machine near at hand, he coolly approached the sentries, chatted with them for a few seconds, and walked on into the enclosure, where he chanced upon a German officer. The latter he plied with polite questions—particularly whether there were any Gotha machines in the sheds and where they were situated.

Having obtained the necessary position, he thanked his informant politely, and strolled back to his machine. A few minutes later he was

15

in the air, and within three he had "fanned-down" sheds and machines to flaming ruins. "Not really a bad stunt," condescended my friend, in conclusion.

"Really, not at all bad," one would agree. In some ways it reminded me of an incident I had been witness to when I was over there myself. For the sake of flying proprieties, we will call him Smith.

Lend your imagination to the scene. A smoke-clouded mess-room; in various recumbent positions, varying degrees of pilots; being British, all silent and painfully shy. As the squadron commander comes in, one—little past schoolboy age—rises from his seat and smartly salutes.

"Oh, you've just come in," says the commander. "I heard you had a fight."

"Yes, sir," replies the boy breathlessly. "B—— and I met six Hun machines. But my gun jammed after half a round. B—— brought down one, I think. I saw it spinning over their lines."

"Where is B——, by the way?" inquires the commander.

"Not back yet, sir," is the reply; "but I saw him cross the lines behind me."

"Engine trouble, I suppose?"

"I don't know. But I say, sir—they were rabbits. They wouldn't even wait."

The squadron commander smiles. The boy resumes his seat with a blush; borrows a cigarette, and is soon buried deep in an illustrated paper. Ten minutes before he was 10,000 or 12,000 feet in the air, fighting for dear life, hopelessly outnumbered.

Ball, Bishop, Guynemer, Hawker, Insall, Robinson, Warneford—it is all the same story. Point of view, of course, depends on how one looks at it. The enemy pins his faith in development of machines only to crumple up helplessly before the daring initiative of British flying youth. These knight-errants of the skies have created a chapter of British history, prouder epic than ever Homer sang.

A short-lived four years of blood-agony has startled a watchful world with an Italian airman delivering a letter, by hand, from his Sovereign to the King of England, a thousand-mile-odd non-stop flight in a frail biplane; a French airman hovering over Berlin; and giant Zeppelins brought flaming to earth by a tiny monoplane and stouter biplanes.

Of the human element, the unsatisfying fragments which every now and then struggle into print convey the barest inkling of the development of the man. That he has developed in his craft is undeniable. But exactly in what manner, or in what particular phase of flying, it is difficult to say. It must be remembered that the Air Service, both in years and experience, is a youthful corps, attracting youth. And, here again, our standardised theories have been sadly distorted in the searching crucible of blood and shell. Youth, invariably, was held to be irresponsible; with warm imagination, but little thought. How clearly the air has negatived that belief.

From intimate acquaintance of young airmen, some successful and some otherwise, I can state that flying develops strength of character and powers of reflection almost abnormally. Perhaps it is that the pursuit of the air is so flavoured with conflicting experiences; in a single flight a man will gain more wisdom and more sound common-sense than in a whole year living under normal conditions on the surface of the earth. Perhaps it is due to the fact of that long grim tussle—and tussle it surely is—that he must wage with Death from the moment he leaves the ground until he has landed safely again.

But I have known youths irresponsible, light-headed, unthinking youths, when they have first reported at a station—develop in a few short weeks into thoughtful, cautious men. The laughter, the gaiety, and care-free attitude was still apparent; but underneath—in that particular part of his mental anatomy that is as sacred to a man as his life—some wonderful change had taken place. In fact, it is common knowledge amongst airmen that the more hours a man spends in the air, the less daring he becomes, the less risk he takes. You never see an "old hand" doing "stunts."

I venture a little story to illustrate my point; meaning, of course, to indicate how necessary in war-flying a man's brain-power has become. Shall we call him Lieutenant B——? There is nothing fictitious about this story. I daresay B—— himself would recognise it at a glance. But there are certain formalities to be observed. "During a fight lasting three hours and forty minutes he successfully registered two siege-batteries on a hostile battery, and observed 100 and 150 rounds respectively." Imagine the skill and thought required to carry out an operation of this nature for so long a time. Imagine the hundred and one little subterfuges in which he had to find resource, to save himself from destruction by hostile anti-aircraft fire or enemy machines.

And a little later: "He made four trips and dropped twelve 112-lb. bombs on two aerodrome objectives. Also, he carried out a large number of successful counter-battery and trench registration shoots under exceedingly unfavourable weather conditions"—it takes a wise man to encounter Nature in her own province, and to get away with it—"and has at all times carried out his duties in a thoroughly keen and able manner, displaying a magnificent spirit of dash and energy."

Amazing are the situations which occur in aerial fighting. And they require all a pilot's thought to extricate himself. Here is one instance, concerning the manner in which a solitary British seaplane beat off the combined attack of five enemy craft, in open fight. With a companion, this pilot had set out from an English coastal base, for reconnaissance patrol.

Somehow, once they got out to sea, they became separated. Seaplane number one was already far ahead, when three German single-seaters dived from the clouds on to the rearmost machine, opening fire from two to three hundred yards. Machine-gun bullets splattered the British machine from all sides. For the time being, all he could do was to keep up a running fight.

Then brains began to tell. Suddenly his machine veered from side to side, in sharp zigzag sweeps. Not only did this manoeuvre serve to put the German gunners off their mark, but also it made it possible for his wireless-operator and engineer to bring their rear guns into play.

Very soon the engineer, with a rapid and accurate "burst," hit the leading enemy machine, and brought him crashing down to the water's edge. The others hesitated; then turned and flew off rapidly towards the Belgian coast. Compare this deed with those of the pilots of the early days.

The 1914 pilot, gallant and daring as he invariably was, was but a puny weakling of his craft compared with his brethren of 1917. Piloting an aeroplane was the last—and only—stage of his education. Operations were carried out after the manner of the privateersmen of the Middle Ages. In one single flight he would combine reconnaissance, bombing, direction of artillery fire, and aerial combat. Such a flight today would end invariably in disaster. Half a mile out from home he would be pounced upon by some enemy fighting-scout, lurking behind the clouds, and his exit would be rapid. Rifle-range often limited his altitude of operations. Now the latest type anti-aircraft guns find targets at a height of over 15,000 feet.

These few facts are written down with no intention of belittling the prowess of those hardy pioneers of the early days, who in courage were giants but in skill little more than children. I remember well one of those early meetings at Hendon, long enough before the war to be forgotten. It was a Sunday usually a field-day of local conception and construction. All manner of quaint "crocks" were wheeled out on to the aerodrome for a try-out. Half the morning would be spent in getting planes and engine attuned. Then the aspiring airman would clamber into his machine. The spectators would surge forward, coaxing and cheering, in the vain delusion that they were at last to witness a real long flight.

Unhappy faith to be so shattered! Away would dance the plane, engine roaring, bounding, and bumping like a giant grasshopper across the unlevel surface of the ground, until, with a last painful effort, she would soar into the air, and come heavily to earth again, a few hundred yards ahead. More tinkering, more bouncing across the ground, and more short-lived leaps. But this unfortunate—and usually costly—amusement was mainly instrumental in paving the way for the aeroplane of today, also the pilot.

Yes, they certainly had pluck, those pioneers. For how else would the hundred antediluvian craft and sixty-six pilots of the original Flying Corps have driven off the systematised attacks of numerous and highly organised squadrons? And of them is related one of the cheeriest yarns of the war. But it will first be necessary for us to carry our minds back from the roaring Flanders battlefield to the comparative seclusion of home.

On a large table in the corner of the grillroom of one of the most fashionable restaurants in London could have been seen, one autumn evening in 1915, the setting for a most sumptuous repast. Other diners were not slow to observe the lavish display of flowers and glitter of wineglasses, and expressed their feelings somewhat pointedly concerning this unnecessary wartime extravagance. The *maître d'hôtel*, cross-examined, was politely discreet. "Merely a party of military gentlemen who desired to celebrate in suitable fashion some anniversary of the war."

With cantankerous references to temporary gentlemen, the pessimists applied themselves to their meals and waited with indignant eyes the arrival of the party. They were not long to arrive. But as the first guest came in, their feelings underwent a sudden change, for he was being pushed by a kindly waiter in a bathchair—a poor maimed figure of a man, without one arm and with both his legs missing, and on the left breast of his khaki tunic he bore the wings of the Flying Corps and the decoration of a Companion of the Distinguished Service Order. The second and third guests were wheeled in in a similar conveyance. The fourth was led in—a great, broad-chested youth, blind in both eyes; while the last two men hobbled painfully across on crutches.

But, at least, if they had paid the dread price of war, they had not lost the happy faculty of enjoying life. The party bubbled over with mirth. Merry peals of laughter rang across the table. Toasts were pledged and toasts drunk. The conversation scintillated with gay quip and happy jest. And whilst many looked on with tear-dimmed eyes, they alone knew it was good to live, good to laugh and joke, good to enjoy the savoury dishes placed before them. For they had earned the right.

Of eight who had crossed in the twilight of that August evening but a year ago, only six remained; the other two had gone to swell the already lengthy Roll of Honour. A year ago, that night they had solemnly pledged that if they were spared, they would meet together at this same dinner-party. Those who could had kept their word. But in that brief twelvemonth had passed a lifetime of unimaginable agony. They had been instrumental in guiding the destiny of two great nations and assuring the sacred safety of the modern civilised world.

CHAPTER 2

A Clear Horizon

Nowadays flying is highly specialised in every branch. The flying commanders are young men, who possess, necessarily, more initiative and imagination than their grey-haired military predecessors. The Army might be content with fitting square pegs into round holes, but in the Flying Corps they believed, and, moreover, insisted, on having the right man in the right place.

For these youthful authorities it required no great mental effort to realise that essentially scientific professions as photography and wireless operating were not matters for hastily trained naval and military men, but rather for civilian experts. Highly necessary it was that these experts should be inculcated with the Service point of view. And to this end they were graduated through a five- to seven-months' course that included instruction in military duties and drills, military aeronautics, a course of technical instruction dealing with engines, construction of aeroplanes, and the theory of flight. They were taught to fly Service machines under Service conditions, aerial tactics, bombing, combat, and artillery observation, after which they were told off as specialists to respective wings.

In the long period of training a man's particular faculty would invariably display itself. Civilian experts were intended throughout for their particular profession. A youngster exhibiting aptitude in bomb-dropping had his attentions officially confined to that matter henceforth; an expert map-reader found himself doomed to reconnaissance for evermore; and—rarest species of all—the aerial fighter passed his days in mock combats in the clouds.

What was the result of this detailed course of instruction? Today, on every front of war, we find the British airman holds the skies. The craft have been specialised with the pilots. There are speedy fighting-scouts, slower and more cumbersome reconnaissance machines, and huge double-engined battleplanes, each with its special purpose. And the modern aeroplane has been developed to such a pitch that it almost flies itself. In fact, it is one of the axioms of fight, when the pilot or his machine has been hit—the best thing to do is to do nothing. "When you're hit, just take your hands off the stick," is the advice of experienced pilots. "If there's sufficient left in her, and you're high enough above the ground, she'll right herself; if not, there's nothing can save her."

On this particular matter my nervous friend waxed almost violent. "What's the use," he complained, "of sitting in a mechanical contraption that works itself, and you're the dummy that pulls the controls? One might as well be a tram-driver. I don't believe even that would be as boring."

I am afraid his viewpoint was somewhat exaggerated. The familiarity of train-travelling has been long enough with us to breed contempt, but not long enough to eliminate an occasional catastrophe. Daily we read of motorcar and tram accidents and collisions at sea, and more and more, unfortunately, of mishaps in the air.

In this manner a certain British pilot had recently the most unnerving experience possible. On the Western front, and flying alongside another machine at an altitude of well over 10,000 feet, he was horrified to see the engine of the other man's machine burst into flame. The fight for life that ensued passes words and imagination. The pilot, who was flying alone, hurriedly tore off his flying-coat, and attempted to beat down the growing flames. The first man could see the yellow, red tongues licking slowly farther and farther towards the pilot's seat, and cursed himself for his own helpless position. He must sit strapped down, while another man was being slowly roasted to death within fifty yards of him.

Suddenly the pilot of the flaming machine seemed to realise that any hope of life was impossible. He smiled, stood up in his machine, then waved his hand and calmly dived overboard into space.

"I have nightmares of that sight to this day," the other pilot told me. "It was too horrible for words."

Principally, specialisation has made possible double the amount of flying in half the time. In the month of September 1917 alone, 285 German aeroplanes were either brought or driven down. That is more in one month than in the entire 1914 campaign.

In the daily communiques we find such extracts as "Ninety-eight bombs were dropped by our aeroplanes during the day on enemy's billets and hutments," or, "Over 10,000 rounds were fired by our aeroplanes from machine-guns at hostile infantry in trenches and shell-holes on the road."

Here in England, we have been raided by Zeppelin and aeroplane, by day and by night, in moonlight and darkness. In the full glare of noon, a squadron of Gothas circled London with all the nonchalance of a practice manoeuvre. What mind could have conceived these happenings, say, four years ago?

Another curious development is that of night-flying. Nowadays, considerably more work is carried out in the air by night than by day. Only a short time ago fourteen giant Capronis, in a flight of over a thousand miles, raided Cattaro by night, and returned without casualty.

On moonlight nights the sky is alive with speeding, phantom shapes. By twos and threes, and sometimes in whole squadrons, the enemy comes creeping over our antiaircraft fire to bomb our hospitals and stretcher-bearers, until British craft flying out to meet them, they make off at top speed. In similar fashion, well-ordered British bombing formations are to be heard—and seen—passing overhead, to disappear later over the enemy's country accompanied by an incessant yapping of anti-aircraft guns. Others fly off singly or in pairs, bound for all manner of strange adventures.

One of these roving commissions chanced upon a hitherto undiscovered enemy aerodrome one night. He planed lower to investigate. The landing-ground was ablaze with light, and there, drawn up in a long line, were a squadron of Gothas about to set out for a bombing expedition in our lines. Half a dozen British bombs were sufficient to destroy at least half the assembled craft and to put off the anticipated raid for a day or so. Then the British pilot calmly proceeded on his original mission.

Meanwhile a couple of kindred craft indulged in the unusual pastime of flying down the main streets of a town at the level of the housetops, firing at bodies of hostile troops, marching up to reinforce their hard-pressed companies in the front-line trenches.

On shore and sea alike war in the air is waged incessantly, by day and by night. Gradually—so gradually as to be almost unnoticeable—the naval pilots have begun to co-operate with their brethren of the Army wing. Formerly the functions of the two Services were entirely dissimilar. Then several squadrons of naval aircraft were loaned to the Western front. So successful was this combination that we find Haig reporting of the R.N.A.S. in the daily *communiqué* that "the pilots have shown energy, gallantry, and initiative, and have proved themselves capable of hard work and hard fighting. Further, the machines with which they are provided have undoubtedly helped largely towards the success of the aerial fighting which has taken place this spring on the front of the British Armies in France."

Of more recent date naval machines have greatly co-operated with General Allenby's Army on the shores of the Holy Land. From the River Wady the unhappy Turk was hurried on to Gaza, from there to Askalon, and he was badly mauled *en route*. A ton of bombs was dropped from a low altitude by one big squadron alone. Also, numerous hits were recorded on two large bodies of troops, numbering about 5,000 of rank and file.

To this naval and military co-operation may be added yet a greater international alliance. America takes the air very seriously. Her battle-cry is "Through the air to Berlin." Already she has allocated £128,000,000 for the immediate construction of 20,000 aeroplanes and the training of 100,000 flying men. With the typical touch of hustle, two of the best engineers in the country were locked together in the room of a Washington hotel for five days, charged with the development of an aeroplane motor for use by American aviators over the battlefields of Europe. They produced the required engine within twenty-eight days.

For over a year the American Lafayette Squadron has been co-operating with the French Flying Corps. The advanced detachment of the American flyers are already in the war area, picking out the lay of the land.

The splendid services of the French have been adequately recounted in the columns of the daily Press, and need but a passing reference here. The giant Italian Caproni has already won worldwide fame. Originally a rather clumsy and awkward craft, the Italians worked away at it so deliberately during the winter that today the Austrians have been driven from the air on every hand.

Stories of the work of these gallant airmen occasionally drift through to this country. The best of such was undoubtedly that of the twenty-year-old Arturo dell' Oro. Twice in aerial combat his machine-gun failed him at the critical moment. And he made a vow that, should such a thing occur again, he would not hesitate to ram his machine into the enemy craft.

The following afternoon an Austrian "Brandenburg" loomed up across the skyline. Up went the youthful airman to attack him. Soaring to a great altitude, he opened fire on his adversary from above. Then the steady "*pit-pit-pit*" of his machine-gun went off as suddenly as it had commenced.

His companions, who were party to his vow, watched anxiously to see what he would do. The Austrian was already making off for his base, when, without hesitation, Arturo put the nose of his machine down at a terrific speed, took the enemy amidships, and both went hurtling to earth from over 10,000 feet.

While, queerest, and certainly most tragic, of the last flights was that of another Italian airman, Olivori. The first of his corps to bring down five enemy machines, which feat permitted him the proud title of "ace," Olivori had added seven to his bag before flying home himself. Fatalistic to a degree was the manner of his last farewell. Laughing and joking with his friends, the conversation suddenly turned upon the recent death of the French champion, Guynemer. At the mention of his name Olivori was observed to go deathly white. He spoke not another word, but walked to his waiting machine and flew off, and had risen barely 200 feet when his engine failed, crashing both pilot and plane to earth.

In the enemy country, more than in any other, aircraft construction is being carried on at fever pitch. Every consideration is being swept away before the deep-throated call of the air-raiding Hun.

Motor-building factories and aeroplane works are enlarging their plant and doubling and trebling their personnel to cope with the influx of orders. The Fokker firm, in particular, have taken over the great Barzina piano factories in Schwerin.

The craft under construction are battle planes, fighting planes (in large numbers), triplanes (remarkable for speed and climbing powers), and heavy three-seated bombers, fitted with 260 h.p. Mercédès, with a climb of 12,000 feet in thirty-five minutes, and capable of carrying 1,700 lb. and 1,800 lb. of bombs.

A species of aerial tank is also under construction. This craft will be built entirely of metal, and is intended for work with the infantry; while a new type of Zeppelin, embodying several new inventions, is being constructed at Friedrichshaven.

Germany lies in the very centre of the air war. France, Belgium, England, and Italy can all attack her from every point of the compass. To meet these deadly attacks the enemy must spread her defensive forces over a very wide area.

The most vital points in their lines of communication—the Rhine bridges—will be at our mercy. They number eighteen in all, with, in particular, the bridges of Cologne, Bonn, Coblenz, and Freiburg. Such important German military positions as Freiburg, Strassburg, Karlsruhe, Mannheim, Cologne, and Essen all lie within easy riding of Nancy.

But whatever is done must be done without delay. Aerial warfare moves with tremendous speed. And such speed is only possible when thought is combined with action. The Allies must hold the mastery of the air, for on it their future national existence depends. And to hold the air we must lay down three craft to every one that Germany constructs.

CHAPTER 3

From Dawn to Twilight

One can only realise the extent of the aerial battle—and battle-field—by studying a largescale map of the entire battle-front, and the use of the imagination. From south of St. Quentin to the North Sea must be at least one aerodrome to every three miles. Kite-balloons dot the line-behind-the-line, three to a mile. Double these estimates, and you have the total number of aircraft of both belligerents working in the air at the same time. The headquarters staffs of both British and German Armies are employing reconnaissance and photographic craft for purposes of information; likewise, army corps and divisional commanders. Kite-balloons and aeroplanes are directing artillery fire. And, for their protection, fighting craft are skimming the clouds, or carrying out semi-personal "hates" and "strafes."

There are no sign-posts or landmarks in the air; neither latitude nor longitude. But, fortunately, some far-seeing map-designer has marked off the contour map-surfaces into alphabetical districts and numerical localities. By this method alone can the geographical positions of the "working" aircraft be decided.

Scores of tiny shapes, thousands of feet up, against the blue sky will be located as being over A1,B2.3, or C3,A6.7. At B4,A2.8 on this particular day an R.A.F. pilot dived on to a German captive-balloon, through a considerable a-a bombardment, and brought it down in flames.

Five miles to the south, another pilot, who had just bombed a railway with agreeable result, was wounded in the arm, and fainted. The dive of his machine brought him round. Again, he took control, but shortly afterwards lost consciousness once more. Eventually, de-spite the pain and the loss of blood, he succeeded in making his own aerodrome The pilot of the consort machine also was hit. But in this case the observer took on, managed to keep the machine level, and flew it until his pilot recovered. Again, the latter fainted. And again, the observer handled the control-stick, managing to land the machine under very difficult circumstances well within our lines.

At B3,A7.5, in the same locality, an officer of the same squadron was effectively demolishing an enemy railway-bridge. Four thousand feet above a British photographer was disturbed at his work by several enemy craft. The fight was short and sweet. One of the intruders went hurtling down to the earth. This decided his companions, and they made off. The photographer "carried on."

In another sector the enemy was making a "push." Our corps, hard pressed, was urgently requiring information as to the deployment of his reserves. Despite the outrageous weather conditions and the fact that several previous attempts had been made for the same reason without success, a pilot essayed the flight from a local aerodrome. This was his second attempt of the day. Profiting from past experience, he flew over at a height of only fifty feet through a murderous rifle and machine-gun fire, and returned with the desired information, still smiling.

I doubt if it is possible to describe adequately the terrors of these same "unfavourable weather conditions" to the reader who has never flown. Let him imagine himself to be in the middle of an open heath, without shelter of hill, tree, or house, and overtaken by a violent thunderstorm. Let him, again, imagine himself to be in that same thunderstorm, 5,000 feet above, in a frail aeroplane, buffeted on all sides by howling winds, trounced with blinding rain and knife-edged hail. In a single recent thunderstorm three British pilots and their machines were hurled to the ground one of them discovered the same evening, eight miles to the south of his course, lying in a field, with both wings shattered, and his engine and fuselage an undistinguishable pulp. But one man got away with it, despite storm and wind and rain.

As the black clouds broke and the jagged flashes of lightning streaked the sky, he was diving down on to a company of enemy infantry. Five miles he was from his own base, with every prospect of being brought down in the enemy's country. Even this failed to daunt him.

Sightless with the driving rain, the Germans fired wildly in all directions. Like a flash he was within fifty feet of them, spluttering their harassed lines from the seething barrels of his machine-guns. Again, he dived, and was hit by a shrapnel fragment. The storm was still raging with bitterest intensity, but he recovered himself. He returned to the charge; diving, climbing up into the storm, and diving again. In all he got rid of between 500 and 600 rounds of bullets. Providence must have set a special guard upon his course that afternoon, for he got home all right.

And here is another *coup de main* of a brother-pilot hidden two miles away in the storm. As the official *Gazette* described it:

"In spite of thunderstorms, and the use of smoke screens by the enemy, he ranged a British gun on a hostile battery position, obtaining eight good hits, destroying two gun-pits and causing a large explosion. He afterwards ranged them on to another battery, destroying a gun-pit, obtained three direct hits on a farm full of troops, and then silenced four batteries."

These are but incidents of the flying man's working day. Between dawn and sunset, they may be doubled, even trebled. Take, as an instance, the record of Captain Trollope, R.A.F. The day was March 24th, 1918, the third of the great German push. His bag included:

Morning—A German two-seater, shot to pieces, in flames; a second two-seater brought down, and a single-seater downed in a spin and seen to crash.

Afternoon—A German two-seater exploded in mid-air.

As he said, in a letter to his parents:

Then I saw two two-seaters very low down; I crashed both of them.

Vice-Commander and Captain John L. Trollope is twenty. And now—though previously reported missing—he is wounded and a prisoner in German hands. His story reads like a romance. He has been through every phase of the war. In June 1915 he was a despatch rider, carrying messages from corps to corps, by motor-cycle. In this way he received his first wound. But, nowise daunted, he transferred to the Naval Wing of the R.A.F., and twelve months to the day was a fully qualified air-pilot. From that time on he was fighting in the air, over the battle-lines, until, in March 1917, he was sent home to instruct pupils.

He was back again in France by March 1918. For in a letter home, he describes to his parents his experiences of a great fight on March 13th, the letter ran:

I had a bullet through both my tanks, and had to glide for the lines. I turned upside-down on landing, landing at some old trenches.

His postscript was characteristic:

But I came out O.K.

Last seen—shortly after dawn on March 28th—he was fighting hard with enemy machines on the eastern horizon.

Four German aeroplanes in ten hours is the day's record of another British pilot, Captain F——. On another occasion, with another pilot, they bagged seven Huns before breakfast, three of them to F——. Another twenty-year-old youth, he has been in France ten months, having brought down over fifty Hun aeroplanes and five kite-balloons, the squadron to which he is attached laying claim to 300 Boche machines.

A squadron is subdivided into flights. Captain F—— led a flight of six pilots for three months, without a casualty. That in itself is a record for war-flying. Once, when fighting a German two-seater, he had the narrowest possible escape. The goggles were shot away from his eyes. In the machine the Verey lights caught fire, setting the woodwork alight. Yet he managed to glide his flaming craft back into his own lines.

And another similar, though somewhat more hazardous adventure befell an observer, some three miles east of the Salient. At 8,000 feet in hot fight, the petrol tanks of a British plane were pierced by machine-gun bullets from a German "Albatross." Despite the extreme danger, the observer got to the tanks, and effected the necessary repairs. Then he noticed that the starboard engine was boiling violently.

At the urgent request of the pilot—who throttled down the engine and slowed speed as much as possible—the observer climbed out on to the lower plane of the wing, clinging desperately with one hand, almost hurled off with the force of the headwind, and effected extensive repairs to the water-circulation system, thus enabling the engine to be opened up to the desired number of revolutions. All this was carried out in a period extending over 105 minutes, and entirely in the open with a wind-force of ninety miles per hour.

CHAPTER 4

The Airman's Log: Some Records of the Skies

The log of the airman is hardly exciting in its official form, but it is when little personal notes come creeping in at the tag of some stereotyped phrase that it grips and thrills. Here is an instance:

Four machines sent up managed to bag five Huns before breakfast.

Another youngster—since brought down by enemy "Archies"—left on record that:

I then went over the German trenches filled with soldiers and was fired on by machine-guns, rifles, and small field-guns, in or out of range!

He landed at the first likely spot he saw—it must be explained that he had been mortally wounded in the interval, and was sinking from loss of blood:—

My machine was badly shot about.

There are logs in history—of the adventurous old sea-captains, roaming the ocean in search of the New World. In words of blood, they were written. Their pages were filled with romance and tragedy, adventures and courage, that no Kipling or Jules Verne could imagine. There is an old brass-clamped volume—long forgotten—that lies in a museum in Madrid, containing the memoirs of Christopher Columbus, the day before he and his adventurous crew sighted that wonderful new land of America.

It runs:

Pray God, that, with tomorrow's dawn may come deliverance. Already the men grow restive, and are threatening to mutiny.

For two days now they have had no food. Unless we sight land soon, I fear they will rise and kill me. But, does such land exist? Is it only some wild fancy of the learned men? I am beginning to fear so.

Then the next day's entry:

Land at last. . . . Yesterday the *Pinta* picked up a piece of wood, rudely carved, and the *Nina* a branch of thorn, with red berries. I wept like a child when first that barren shore showed up through the sea-mist. When the call of the watch went up, 'Land ahoy!' the sailors did but laugh at him. But as he did persist, they crowded to his side. Now, they are busy planning the conquest of this unknown shore; and dreaming of what they will do once we have landed. For myself, my heart is bowed down with the weight of my exceeding joy.

Of Scott slowly starving to death in the great snow-bound waste of the Antarctic, we remember that last message to the country found in his log, written:

For my own sake I do not regret this journey, which has shown that Englishmen can endure hardship, help one another, and meet death with as great a fortitude as ever in the past. . . . We have no cause for complaint, but bow to the will of Providence, determined still to do our best to the last.

And his reference to "that very gallant gentleman," Captain Gates, who walked out into the snow, so that he should no longer be a burden to his starving companions.

There have been other very gallant gentlemen who have flown off with the twilight, never to return. What happened to them, none can say. But sometimes their logs have been found, filled in to the moment when they must have been hit and their aeroplane plunged headlong for the earth. Sometimes, on these tattered records will be found an ugly brown smudge; that tells its own story, but too eloquently. A captain of the R.F.C. went out one day early in the war, to make a long flight over the enemy country. On the way out he was hit by shrapnel, and his thigh was shattered. This much he tells us in his report:

I was wounded, but determined to keep on, as the reconnaissance was of the most vital importance.

The report went on almost to the moment of landing. Then his machine crumpled to pieces; and he was found dead. The report—the log—apologised that he could not finish it, as he was "so weak and faint from loss of blood."

The modern log of the flying man differs little from that of the master mariner. It does not tell of seas and shores and hidden rocks. Instead, there is something, if possible, more fascinating. It recounts wonderful adventures: racing through the clouds, diving down to the earth at hundreds of miles an hour, plunging and rocking in a sudden thunderstorm, battling for dear life against the mighty winds of the skies.

It is the unvarnished narrative of what Lloyd George referred to—on that historic occasion in the House of Commons, when moving a vote of thanks to the Flying Services—as where:

The heavens are their battlefields. They are the cavalry of the clouds. High above the squalor and the mud, so high in the firmament that they are not visible from earth, they fight out the eternal issues of right and wrong. Their struggles there by day and night are like a Miltonic conflict between the winged hosts of light and darkness.

A young naval pilot refers in his log to one of these battles in the heavens:

When at 11,000 feet I saw ten Gothas coming inland. I climbed up to them and engaged one on the right of the formation about three miles out to sea at something over 12,000 feet. Fired a hundred rounds from straight behind his tail at a hundred yards range; bullets were seen to enter the Gotha's fuselage. The machine started into a slow spin. I followed and fired about twenty-five more into him to make sure. My gun then jammed, and in trying to clear I got into a very fast spin with my engines on. Got out of this in time to see the enemy crash into the sea, I then landed, had my gun-jam cleared, and I went up after the remaining eight Gothas—one had been shot down in flames in the interval—and caught up with them at 14,000 feet and engaged them in turn from above and below. Then devoted all my attention to one Gotha, and after firing 200 rounds into him, silenced both his guns. I think both the German gunners must have been hit, as I was able to get within sixty feet of him without being fired at. I finally ran him out of ammunition.

The following extract is of a very different nature. It is from the log of Paul Pavelaka, a young American with one of the most romantic stories of the war. Previously he was a gipsy, tramping the United States. He was twenty-six when he died. He beat his way round the globe and halfway back again, whereupon he ran into the war. He got a wound fighting Huns with the Foreign Legion, and the *Croix de Guerre* fighting Huns in the sky with the American Escadrille. On this occasion he missed being burnt to death in a flaming aeroplane by what was almost a miracle. Here is his story:

> I was at about 10,000 feet when I first became conscious of a slight smell of burning. When I looked towards the petrol-tank, I discovered a tiny flame licking round the base. From then on it was a nightmare. All that I was conscious of was a sudden rush of smoke and flame. Hurriedly I put her down towards the earth. And, as I did so, the flame beat almost into my face. It seemed like an eternity before I got down. And I only accomplished that with a smashed wing and a broken propeller. I was pretty well dazed for hours afterwards.

There has always been considerable uncertainty as to the manner in which that "ace" of British airmen, Captain Ball, V.C., met his death. It has now been described in the record of the celebrated Captain von Richthofen, who is credited by the Germans with having brought down sixty-four Allied aeroplanes.

This doughty airman wrote in his log:

> It was my brother to whom this signal honour fell. The famous Captain Ball—by far the best English flying man—was his twenty-second adversary. The equally well-known Major Hawker I had already taken to my bosom some months earlier. It gave me special joy that it should be my brother's luck to down the second of England's champions.
>
> Captain Ball was flying a triplane, and encountered my brother alone at the front. Each one tried to grip the other, and neither exposed his vulnerable part. It proved a brief encounter. Neither of the two succeeded in getting behind the other.
>
> Suddenly within the brief moment of mutual frontal attack both managed to fire some well-aimed shots. Both flew at one another; both fired. Each had a motor before him, and the chances of a hit were very slender, the speed being double as great as the normal. There was really little probability of either

hitting the other.

My brother, who was somewhat lower, had banked his machine too much, and he lost his balance. For a few moments his machine was beyond control. Very soon, however, he regained command, but found that his opponent had shot both his petrol tanks to pieces. To land was, therefore, the only resource.

Quickly! Out with the plug or the body will burn! The next thought was; 'What has become of my opponent?' At the moment of canting he had observed how the enemy also had swerved aside. He could, therefore, not be very far from him. The question arose: 'Is he over or under me?' He was below. My brother saw the triplane swerving again and falling ever more deeply: Captain Ball fell and fell until he reached the ground. He was in our territory.

Both adversaries had in the brief moment of their encounter hit each other with their powerful machine guns, and Captain Ball had received a shot in the head.

He had on him some photographs and newspaper cuttings from his home country in which he was greatly praised. He appeared shortly before to have been home on leave.

During Boelke's time Captain Ball had destroyed thirty-six German machines. Now he, too, had met his master—or was it a coincidence that a great one such as he should also die the usual hero's death?

Captain Ball was without doubt the leader of the anti-Richthofen squadron, and I believe that now the Englishmen will prefer to abstain from trying to catch me. I am sorry for this, because thereby we are robbed of many a fine opportunity for giving the English a jolly drubbing.

Had not my brother been wounded, I believe he would, on my return from leave also have been granted his leave with fifty-two Englishmen to his credit.

A somewhat similar vain glorious recital is to be found in the private diary of a member of the crew of one of the Zeppelins which raided England in 1915. It commences with the receipt of a telegraphic order from Berlin:

Weather favourable; attack London tonight, (and continues) Punctual to the minute *L33* leaves its hiding-place, the motors begin to hum, the ship rises majestically and we are off—

against England. . . .

The day was ending when the steersman reported: "Twenty-six miles from the coast." Then:

Land in sight. We recognised Yarmouth, and then the ships separated to avoid collisions in the darkness.

A couple of minutes later the wireless operator brought the information that the English had sparked, "Zeppelins over the Wash!"

At 12.15 we were over the Thames to the west of London. Then, 'Full speed ahead.' Suddenly a number of searchlights began to work ahead of us. Shrapnel and shells burst all around the ship—the *L33*—but it came safely through, and we saw her bombs dropping on the city, and fires breaking out at various points.

Meanwhile we had reached the suburbs. '*Klas zum Warfen*' and then '*Abwerfer!*' are the commands, but in the same moment a searchlight catches us. The first bomb falls and others follow at short intervals. In spite of the hum of the propellers and the noise of the motors, we can hear the bombs exploding, and the shrapnel in our neighbourhood.

At 1.15 we crossed the coast-line, and at 2.30 this message was sparked: 'Place North Hinder Lightship. London attacked.'

The airman's log embraces earth and sky, cloud and trench and sea alike. In that breezy vernacular of the air, it whispers apologetically of "stunts" and "buses," "bumps" and "planes"; it pictures badly winged craft battling for life against the horizon of the skyline; and also, of long, dreary watches over the grey wastes of the seas.

The romance and daring of these flights find full flavour in a few—often ill-spelt—words. The phrasing lacks nothing of the picturesque. Refreshingly original is the wording, and the matter smacks of clear heavens and sparkling skies.

In the log—irreverently termed "gamebook"—one comes across such phrases as:

Number Three was troubled by a searchlight and dived for it. Sliding down the beam, he smashed it up effectively.

Then the stern eye of authority commenced to frown on such levity. Orders were issued that the words "plane" and "bus" were no longer to be employed in official reports when referring to an aeroplane. "Laying the eggs," "getting pipped," and "doing a stunt" were less desirable expressions than dropping the bombs, being wounded, or making a flight.

For the guidance of future offenders, a schedule was drawn up. Worded in choice official phraseology, the average report now reads somewhat after the following manner:

> 7.20 a.m., 8,000 feet, B,A2.7 over the trenches; considerable activity in the enemy reserved trenches. Two pill-boxes observed, B,A3.9, also a tank trap, covered by planks, tree branches, and gravel. 7.30, 9,000, train, locomotive and five coaches, proceeding westerly direction between S—— and M——, (and so forth.)

All of which the Flying Services "chewed over" round their mess-tables and around bleak aerodromes. Until, finally, if not turning a blind eye thereon, at least winked at barefacedly.

And, somehow, that personal note would come creeping into their reports. The breezy nonchalance, the genuine joy of the profession, would not be denied. Thus, we find one hardy adventurer:

> I came down to 2,500 feet, and continued my descent at a rate of well over 100 miles an hour. At about 1,000 feet I loosed my bombs all over the place. The whole way down I was under fire—two anti-aircraft in the yard, guns from the fort on either side, rifle fire, machine guns, and, most weird of all, great bunches of what looked like green rockets, but I think they were flaming bullets. My chief impression was the great speed, the flaming bullets streaking by, the incessant rattle of the machine-gun and rifle fire, and one or two shells bursting close by, knocking my machine all sideways and pretty nearly deafening me. . . . My eyes must have been sticking out of my head like a shrimp. I banked first on one wing-tip and then on the other, now slipping outwards, and now up and down. I covered, I suppose, getting on for 250 miles. Have not yet heard what damage was done. The C.O. was awfully braced!

Perhaps pardonable under the circumstances.

> I was using the bow gun and was leaning over when he came out right under me. . . I shot him, and the machine went into a nose-dive.

Thus, a United States naval airman has it written in his private record concerning a fight in the North Sea, with five Hun machines, in which he participated. He wrote:

Three of us were on patrol in the morning, and just beyond the North Hinder five Huns drove on our tails. We fought for forty-five minutes, and in the middle of it a submarine bobbed up right under me. We had all dropped our bombs at the start of the fight, so that all I could do was to give him a few shots which drove the hatch closed and the boat to duck.

Well, it was a running fight. The chief picked two crews that he felt confidence in, and I was picked. We had orders to keep our bombs, to run from nothing, no matter what the odds were against us, and to show the Hun that we could fight. Nice start for a party. So out we went and ran on to five Huns sitting in the water near their coast. They jumped up and we went for them.

We started with a stern action and we were landing too hot for them. They fell into a circle as quick as you could wink and circled below us. We simply riddled them and they did the same for us. One tried to cross our bow to ram us, but misjudged, and as we held on he had to go below us.

I was using the bow gun and was leaning over when he came out right under me, with the gunner who sat aft looking at me and pointing his gun in my face. I shot him, and the machine went up on its ear and into a nose-dive. It levelled out just at the water and withdrew. I don't know how much damage was done. We had no time to look.

Then my pilot rushed the remains of the circle and broke it up. They ran away in column ahead, but again this put us at an advantage, so they formed a higher and larger circle and really started to 'lay us cold.'

My wireless man, who was using a rear gun, was shot through the neck, and my gun had got so hot by then that the sights had rolled off, and I took what ammunition I had left and crawled back over the lower plane.

They saw me crawling in and made it quite hot. Luckily for me, I slipped on his blood and missed a very good burst that was meant for my head. Then I used his gun until we 'had put it over them,' and our ammunition ran low.

We used 2,500 rounds between the two machines. Most of the action was at 200 feet.

It was a regular bull-dog fight and very dirty work. We made them change their minds, I think. It was the best fight we ever put up from this station, and the first pilots of the machines simply 'stuck them in to it.' The air was literally full of lead and traces of smoke.

But don't run away with the idea that the Hun won't fight. He had no idea of letting us get away with it that I could see.

In other instances, the log would assume more impersonal a note. Squadron and wing commanders would report of Flight-Sub-Lieut. X. or Captain Y. that:

He ambushed three aeroplanes from a cloud, dived at them, and then, suspecting a trick, zoomed up to find three fighting planes diving at him from higher clouds. Though below them, he accepted the challenge, and at once doubled up the first one he met."

He attacked a formation of fifteen hostile machines returning from a raid on England. Closing on one machine, he engaged it at close quarters and sent it in a nose-dive into the sea.

And of another pilot, unknown, that:

After a long chase he engaged and brought down one of the enemy raiders returning from England. He engaged a second, but his gun jammed, and though he continued the pursuit to the enemy coast, he could not clear his gun.

While, at sea, the R.N.A.S. has on record that:

They fight when they must, and the straightest shot wins. If hit, unless hopelessly out of control, they take to the water like a wounded duck. If the damage is beyond temporary repair, they sit on the surface and pray for the dawn and a tow from a friendly destroyer.

Here, on the other hand, is the version of a German airman participating in one of these raids on Great Britain. He is Watch Officer Senior Lieutenant of the Naval Reserve Grener. As they approach the British coast in the twilight, he records in his log:

The English coast must come into sight any moment. Sure

enough, there it is in sharp outline. Soon we shall be near enough to recognise where we are. . . . Slowly, quite slowly, we approach it. Once in a while a cloud intervenes. But as yet all is quiet and peaceful. Now the coast lies perpendicularly beneath us. Now, now at last we near the goal of our desires.

The English are waiting for us!

We don't intend to be kept out. Tonight, we have time. The night is longer than in June. So, on we go. Now and then a searchlight picks us up. Now and then a shot flares at us. . . But, notwithstanding, there it is—quite plainly—our goal—London. Thou city of my dreams—the cause of my sleepless nights! . . . A brilliant wreath of searchlights betokens the prize from afar. The captain consults his map and compass, and then commands, 'Cross London from north to south and then veer to the east.' . . . Beneath us we can see and hear that our presence is detected. We discern masked lights. Others burst forth and go out. They are the muzzle-flashes of the anti-aircraft guns. Searchlights stab the sky, first slowly, carefully, anxiously, then wildly, from this, then from that side. Sometimes they locate nothing but a drifting cloud. But now they have found us. Even oftener and more accurately the ghostly white stabs of light are directed straight at our craft and envelop us. Suddenly it gleams bright as day.

Now shrapnel is bursting fiercely all around us. Shells are tearing at us like birds of prey with flaming eyes. Fore and aft, below us, above us, everywhere, they scream and roar. It is hellish, yet beautiful. And loud above the crash of the thundering shells we hear the deep bass of our faithful bombs—*bum—bum—bum*— and always the orchestral accompaniment to the concert supplied by our whirring propellers.

But we are doing things in London, too. There, on our starboard, is a mighty cave-in; and there, to port, another. In their proximity, where a fourth bomb has dropped, there is a whole series of explosions. Heavens, but we're letting them have it this time! There is comrade von L—— at work. He has peppered London before. Only tonight he is less excited.

But things are getting too hot for us. Away from this inhospitable neighbourhood. A caressing west wind is at our back, and amid protecting clouds we start on our return journey to the coast. Here another, still heavier but futile bombardment awaits us. We've been so busy that nobody had time to remember that our visit to England tonight has been in freezing cold. Our artificial breathing apparatus is almost glued to our lips by the Arctic frost. But it's warmer now. Gradually our nerves and lungs resume their normal functions. Home coasts beckon to us, and before we know it, we're safe again and landing on friendly soil.

There are many sides of the airman's work which have been recounted in this short chapter, but few of the possibilities. The "log" of the air-pilot goes to make a breathless, fascinating chapter of war, an epic of history.

Chapter 5

A Page of History

The finest of all war-reading is to be discovered in the award pages of *The London Gazette.*

It is the more interesting because it is scrupulously correct in every detail. There is a plain-told narrative, without attempt at fiction or exaggeration. Deed follows deed, in short, terse sentences, with a variety that is at once fascinating and bewildering. Here is a single page from a single list of awards: Military Crosses, Distinguished Service Orders, bars to D.S.O., and D.S.C.s. Almost intentionally, the reports of the various Wing-Commanders of the R.A.F. must have been culled each of their finest stories, and strung together in a dazzling line. But, judge for yourselves.

The first deed—it comes under the list of D.S.O.s—is the story of an Homeric combat, in the mist, between a British fighter and a German Albatross.

Apparently for some time these two had been hunting round, and out of sight of one another. Then the mist lifted, and they passed within eighty yards. The enemy was first in with his shot, and getting our pilot through the heart, killed him instantly. The former closed in to administer the *coup de grâce*; but he had counted without the British observer. The machine was already going down, with the Albatross hard behind it, when the observer managed to crawl across his companion's dead body to the control-stick.

Though wounded in the hand, he drove the enemy plane off with his gun, and got his own machine under control. Thus, he continued over the lines, and crashed within a mile of his own aerodrome. Even then, dazed and wounded as he was, he insisted on being taken on to his corps headquarters to report. "He showed great coolness and skill," is the laconic comment.

This, again, in the concluding remark of the next award. However, we have here the history of a few startling weeks, told in as few lines.

"For courage and initiation." This particular pilot displayed even more than these two sterling qualities. Rather let it be said that he possessed determination and staying power to an unusual degree. By day and by night, in fine weather and in storm, he kept at it incessantly. He led offensive patrols, which "under his able and determined leadership consistently engaged enemy aircraft"; set fire to and destroyed enemy kite-balloons, and constantly brought down German planes out of control.

On one occasion he attacked a new type enemy two-seater machine. Immediately the Hun dived steeply to the east. Our man, following hard on his tail, closed on it, firing a long burst at close range. As the report says, "the enemy went down vertically out of control." But perhaps his finest "stunt" was when "he attacked an enemy kite-balloon at night, and destroyed both the balloon and its shed by fire."

Then, almost before one can get one's breath, there follow the adventures of an airman who possessed the unique faculty of "never failing to locate enemy aircraft." And having nosed them out, he always attacked without any regard to the numbers against him. In nine short weeks he was successful in bringing down nine enemy aircraft—an average of one machine per week. This, let it be said, at nineteen years of age: "a magnificent fighter."

It is an uncertain life; but that is its greatest charm. At a height of over 18,000 feet one pilot attacked and destroyed an enemy two-seater reconnaissance machine. In the trenches there happen adventures, many and varied; but one can be certain of them—to a degree. Nothing is certain in the guerilla warfare of the clouds. It is single combat all the time—man to man, gun to gun; and the better man gets away with it. There are no reserves to be rushed up to his support, no unfair preponderance of heavy artillery.

This same pilot, on another occasion, attacked single-handed six enemy triplanes, bringing one down and driving off the remainder. Another carried out some very useful and long flights in flying machines of an old type in East Africa. He completed his reconnaissances even when the machine had been practically uncontrollable through the "bumps." "He has been eager and ready to go up at all times, and has shown no thought of personal danger."

And yet another, "when attacked on artillery patrol by eight enemy aircraft, succeeded in driving down one machine, the rest being driven off east."

Halfway down the page we come across the story of a fight, close-in, at seventy-five yards' machine-gun range. The Britisher opened the engagement, nose on, firing rapidly. They turned and climbed and dived awhile, each man fighting for the "upper berth." For, once there, the uppermost pilot has his opponent in his "blind spot," and at his mercy. Opportunity came at last; there followed a murderous burst; the German turned over on its side and commenced to spin. He was followed, and engaged at thirty yards' range. It was the end of that perfect day. With a last uncontrollable lunge, the Hun dived down into the interminable space below.

One would have thought that sufficient sensation for the day. But late in the afternoon, and again on patrol, this same British pilot took on no less than fourteen Albatross at one time. He followed one of them to 8,000 feet, firing all the time. The official *Gazette* says:

This is confirmed by other pilots of the patrol to have fallen completely out of control.

So, the terse accounts run on, each new one putting the last out of countenance. For a second bar to his Distinguished Service Cross, an R.A.F. youngster put in an unusually hustling day. In aerial combat, alone, in the grey hours of the early dawn, he ran up against a new type twin-tailed two-seater enemy machine, firing a good many rounds at point-blank range. The enemy machine dived; but again, he attacked, until, eventually, the Boche went down vertically with his engine full on. The wings came off, and the machine was observed to crash.

Later in the same day he observed two formations of ten and five Albatross scouts respectively. He attacked one of the enemy machines and sent it down in a flat spin, and falling over sideways, completely out of control. And, almost as an afterthought, he led out an offensive patrol, towards sunset, adding yet another Hun to his personal bag.

To a highly suitable climax, the story of Temporary Second Lieutenant P——:

Whilst on artillery patrol his machine was attacked by a hostile scout. Although he was wounded by the first burst of hostile fire, he continued to work his gun, and succeeded in driving off the enemy machine, which is believed to have been severely damaged. When taken to the C.C.S. he insisted on being sent to his squadron, in order to make a reconnaissance report on movement behind the enemy's lines. After doing this he was taken back to the C.C.S., where he was operated on and the bullet extracted. This officer has proved himself a most reliable observer. He has done consistent good work, and many of his reports have been of the greatest value.

CHAPTER 6

The Dawn Patrol

The reconnaissance "bus" lay, herded with her kind, in a corner of the bleak aerodrome, within a circle of crude flares, and against the adventure pregnant blackness of the early morning. The forlorn array of cans that lay scalped around her; the fresh odour of oil and spirit— a combination flavour peculiar to aircraft; the tense hum of many voices; the muffled figure of the pilot, hard by; the sudden booming of the mighty engine heralded a speedy departure.

With her squat, blunt nose and broad wing-spread she stood, a craft apart from the slimmer, more graceful fighting scouts. A double-engine battleplane, her triple fuselages interposed by a serviceable, albeit sinister-looking gun-pit, towered over her, in the background, almost with an air of condescension. A toy, in proportion, a Bristol bullet squatted alongside, and a little in rear of her. The reconnaissance bus was the last in line of six similar craft, squatted across the landing-ground, barely distinguishable in the half-lights, their present muteness proclaiming a separate mission.

The pilot clambered aboard—one foot on the wing, and over the side of the fuselage, into his seat. His observer was already crouched in the forward pit; his head visible only, and that successfully camouflaged by a pair of unsightly goggles. To a sudden motion of the pilot's hand the blocks were jerked out from the wheels, and the machine lunged forward.

Circling gracefully overhead, she could be seen dipping spasmodically to the rarefied patches of air that the growing light had churned up out of the mist-laden depths of the previous night. Then she turned her nose due east, and commenced to climb gradually. And gradually, as she merged into the low-lying clouds, the silhouette of her outline grew less and less distinct. To the pilot, the aerodrome became a mere black smudge against the grey background of the surface.

As he gained altitude, the dawn-light widened; rolling back, like a coverlet, the landscape of the earth beneath, as far as eye could reach, to the north, to the sand-fringed sweep of blue waters.

The slumbering armies of land and sea woke to animation. Bare reaches of the ribbon-like roadways darkened, here and there, with painfully crawling masses. With a quick puff of white smoke, a great gun spoke somewhere far below. Against the distant skyline the low hull of a destroyer loomed into view.

Presently they swept across the lines, to the accompaniment of a desultory antiaircraft bombardment. As the minute, flame-grey patches commenced to flick the sky in unhealthy proximity, the pilot "stuffed her nose down," and she streaked out of range. This method having proved effective, he then determined to regain his height—a highly judicious factor in the unequal combat betwixt gun and plane. The rush of upward air died away perceptibly.

The angle of transit veered from fifteen below to fifteen above the horizontal. The decrease in speed waxed significant. Then he found time to make his map-readings. Two highways flung outwards, like the arms of a tuning-fork. In the far distance a turning, twisting roadway completed a wide triangle. Immediately below, another roadway ran left and right at a sharp right angle. A group of small houses straggled along either side to the distance of some half a mile. In rear of the village a gleaming railroad track curved into view. Too far to the north! He changed his course accordingly.

Before him he caught a glimpse of his observer, head bent well forward, pencil in hand, busy over his report sheet. It was too early yet for any considerable activity with road and canal traffic. Behind Langemarck, their sloping wooden roofs painfully conspicuous, nestled a township of huts. Down the railway, from the north-east, steamed a train—like a worm wriggling across the mud. The observer noted the direction, counted the number of trucks, spied further for rolling stock on sidings, and then made a note on his pad:

5.30 a.m., 10,000 feet, 9, A5. 3, troop train proceeding westerly direction: one locomotive and twelve coaches.

Then his roaming eye caught and held the landmarks of their objective. Somewhere between Roulers and Oostnieuwkerke, south of the connecting high-road and hidden in a little wood, lay the emplacement he was ordered to locate. He startled his pilot from his reverie with a loud "Hulloa!" on the speaking-tube.

"What's the matter?" came the quick response.

"Will you go lower," the observer demanded curtly.

Obedience was to perform the easiest known feat in aviation circles. The dial hand on the face of the altimeter veered rapidly downward.

As the earthward rush developed, the surface grew more distinguishable. Roads and railways, rivers and canals, towns and villages jumbled together in uncanny profusion. Now the long-sought wood was easily visible. For a moment or so they circled it at a low altitude, the observer, with his glasses gripped to his eyes, leaning far across the side. Then the speaking-tube broke the tension again. "Home, Jeames," was its brief comment, as an anti-aircraft battery opened rapid fire from somewhere behind the town.

And at that moment—in flying parlance—they "ran right into it." The shock of the burst took the frail aeroplane with a strange, almost human quivering. The smoke and the stench beat into their faces, filling their eyes and lungs, almost choking them. Unconsciously they were aware of the unpleasant rip-rip of shrapnel bullets piercing the taut fabric of the wings. Dark, gleaming lights flashed suddenly before their eyes. The machine commenced to perform the queerest and most absurd antics. Round they swept in a breathless semi-circle, diving from that into a dark, abysmal space. The rush of upward air roared into their ears, filling the head with a strange drumming. Earth and sky alike were intermingled in a swiftly moving kaleidoscope.

At 2,000 feet, by superb airmanship, the pilot "got her out" and on a level keel again. With his engine at top speed, he made off in the direction of the lines.

The ensuing twenty minutes, preliminary to regaining their height, was an unnerving and an anxious period. But gradually the machine commenced to climb, and by the time the lines were reached the machine skirted over at a respectful height. They were taking no unnecessary risks.

The subsequent report, perused by the Wing Commander, contained, beyond the customary routine observations, no further reference to the adventure than:

Over X—— we encountered an intensive antiaircraft bombardment.

CHAPTER 7

Some V.C.s of the Air

When, in 1856, Queen Victoria founded the crimson ribbon of chivalry, with attached the tiny Maltese cross of metal made from Russian cannon taken at Sebastopol, and bearing the prized inscription, "For Valour," it was thought adequate to meet any possible deed of human pluck and endurance. But that was before the days of the Flying Service. Though they would be the last to admit it. They hate advertisement!

"Every airman should have a V.C.," remarked, the other day, a gushing member of the fairer sex.

Another woman demanded of that good fellow and splendid airman Guynemer, "Now that you have won every possible decoration, including those foreign 'crosses,' what other cross can you win?"

"The wooden cross, madam," was his prompt and courteous reply.

Try it on any airman of your acquaintance. His reply would be somewhat similar, but hardly polite.

To a degree this outspoken—and most genuine—admiration is permissible. Really, these youthful heroes of the skies have bewildered and dazzled the prosaic old world that works and fights beneath their speeding feet, beyond understanding. The "nut"—pre-war despised—the sportsman, the gunner, the ne'er-do-well, the soldier are numbered in their ranks. Their courage has made our hearts leap. Their daring and gallantry have made the horrors of bloody war almost worth the while. They have put history to shame, and dwarfed the *Odyssey* of Homer to insignificance. Though perhaps the latter supplied the words lacking to the *Paean*, when he wrote:

> *. . . sails*
> *The aerial space, and mounts the winged gales:*
> *O'er earth and ocean wide prepared to soar,*
> *The dreaded arm a beamy javelin bore,*
> *Ponderous and vast: which, when her fury burns,*

Proud tyrants humbles, and whole hosts o'erturns.

Here are a few phrases, chosen at random, from the tales which follow on. They speak for themselves!

On returning with a damaged machine he had always to be restrained from immediately going out on another.

Five others then attacked him at long range, but these he dispersed on coming to close quarters.

And:

On starting the return journey, he was mortally wounded, but succeeded in flying for thirty-five minutes to his destination, and reported the successful accomplishment of his object.

Again:

Though suffering extreme torture from burns, he showed the most conspicuous presence of mind in the careful selection of a landing-place.

And, yet again:

He descended at a safe distance from the burning machine, took up Sub-Lieutenant Smylie, in spite of the near approach of a party of the enemy, and returned to the aerodrome—a feat of airmanship that can seldom have been equalled for skill and gallantry.

First of them all must be related the incidents of the two latest flying V.C.s, and incidentally the first to be awarded to the newly-formed Royal Air Force. The story of Lieutenant Alan McLeod, described as "an indomitable fighter," is unparalleled in the history of the air. Though five times wounded, he beat off the attack of eight German triplanes. His machine was in flames, but he succeeded in piloting it back, almost to the British lines. His observer had been wounded in the fight, and was unable to extricate himself from the burning wreckage. McLeod immediately came to his aid, and only when he was certain that his companion was in comparative safety did he give thought to his own wounds. Then he fainted off from exhaustion and loss of blood.

Flying at a height of 5,000 feet, attacking hostile formations with bombs and machine gun, these eight enemy craft had dived at them from all directions. The situation seemed hopeless. Eight enemy guns ranged on the British machine—overhead, beneath the tail, and on either side. An ordinary pilot would have gone down. But McLeod was no ordinary pilot. Manoeuvring rapidly and with great skill, he turned his plane first in one direction, then in another. Thus, the observer was enabled to fire rapid "bursts" at each enemy machine in turn, bringing down three of them out of control.

Meanwhile, McLeod had sustained no fewer than five wounds—the observer, six. A German bullet had penetrated the petrol tank of his machine, setting it on fire. Yet, despite his condition, and despite the desperate position they were in, he unstrapped his belt and climbed out on to the bottom plane of the left wing. There he controlled his machine from alongside the body, and, banking her over at a sharp angle, he kept the flames to one side. Thus manoeuvring, he enabled the observer to continue his gunfire until, eventually, they crashed to earth in "No Man's Land."

There the fire broke out with renewed intensity. The observer was still in the flaming machine. But McLeod fought his way through smoke and flame, and dragged him from the burning wreckage. All the time he was under heavy machine-gun fire from the enemy lines, and in constant danger from the explosion of his own bombs. In fact, one of these did go off and wounded him for the sixth time.

A single-handed battle with an enemy aerodrome and nineteen German aeroplanes, from a height of only fifty feet above ground, was the adventure that gained for Lieutenant Alan Jerrard, R.A.F., the second Cross. According to the *Gazette*:

When on an offensive patrol with two other officers he attacked five enemy aeroplanes, and shot one down in flames, following it down to within 100 feet of the ground, and, engaging single-handed some nineteen machines, which were either landing or attempting to take off, succeeded in destroying one of them, which crashed on the aerodrome. A large number of machines then attacked him, and whilst thus fully occupied he observed that one of the pilots of his patrol was in difficulties. He immediately went to his assistance, regardless of his own personal safety, and destroyed a third enemy machine.

Fresh enemy machines continued to rise from the aerodrome, which he attacked one after another, and only retreated, still engaged with five enemy machines, when ordered to do so by his patrol leader. Although apparently wounded this very gallant officer turned repeatedly and attacked singlehanded the pursuing machines, until he was eventually overwhelmed by numbers and driven to the ground.

Somewhat different was the manner in which Major Bishop, D.S.O.—the British Immelmann, as our friend the Hun describes him—was awarded the coveted Cross. It was more for a single brilliant action than work over a continued period, although the latter included the destruction of forty enemy aeroplanes, and several kite-balloons, and the deed that won him the D.S.O.:

While in a single-seater he attacked three hostile aeroplanes, two of which he brought down, although in the meantime he was himself attacked by four other hostile machines.

Bishop is the son of the registrar of a small town in Ontario, Canada. Only nineteen years of age, in his first fifty-seven air-fights he brought down twenty-one German aeroplanes and two balloons. His appearance gives every indication of the great physical courage and determination necessary to a pilot with such a record. He is well built, with open, resolute face, cleanshaven, and a quiet, almost subdued manner.

The particular exploit for which he was awarded the V.C. was described by Mr. Roland Hill as follows:

Once he swooped down from above the clouds, to find, twelve miles behind the line, a brand-new aerodrome, with eight nice, new Albatross machines on a nicely plotted lawn. "His sudden appearance upset the Germans' luncheon, so he politely spiralled up behind the airsheds, and when the first machine started up, swooped down on its tail at about fifty feet, through a spray of machine-gun bullets, and sent it crashing down completely wrecked, its pilot killed. Turning again, he swept the second Albatross, as it was just starting up, and saw it catch fire. Climbing up to about 1,000 feet, every kind of gun popping away at him, he found the third machine getting under way, and swiftly raced after it.

One little scrap in the air, and he caught it with the full blast of his machine gun and sent it side-slipping into a clump of trees. The fourth machine, by this time, was climbing to get the advantage of height, so he followed suit, and a three or four minutes' chase in the air resulted. The German turned to give battle when the fifth machine was also well under way, and they seemed to have our man sandwiched. But the British airman kept at Number Four until he had the satisfaction of seeing him flutter down completely out of control. He was just in a favourable position to grab the fifth Albatross when his ammunition gave out, so he waved a farewell with the empty drum and started for home.

Shortly after the award of his Cross, he returned to Canada for a few months' spell as an instructor in a large training-school. During this period, he was married to Miss Margaret Eaton Burden, daughter of Mr. C. E. Burden, and niece of Sir John Eaton. After which he returned to France, to command a squadron. Additional to the former decorations he has also been awarded the Military Cross, received the personal congratulations of Sir Douglas Haig, and his father has been congratulated by Sir Robert Borden, the Canadian Premier. (*Vide Winged Warfare* by William Bishop, An Ace over the Western Front—in his own words: Leonaur, 2011.)

Bishop's was the thirteenth bronze cross awarded to the Flying Services. Among other decorations they had already annexed, by the end of 1916, no less than 7 V.C.s, 72 D.S.O.s, 304 M.C.s, 97 M.M.s, 54 D.C.M.s, 53 Meritorious Service Medals, and 436 mentions in despatches.

Perhaps the most daring of these incidents was that of Richard Bell Davies, V.C., D.S.O., R.N., a squadron commander in the R.N.A.S. Setting out with Flight Sub-Lieutenant Smylie in two bombing machines for an air attack on Ferrijik railway-junction, in the Gallipoli Peninsula, at the dawn of a summer day, Smylie's machine was hit and brought down by a violent anti-aircraft bombardment. The pilot planed down over the station, releasing all his bombs except one, which failed to drop, simultaneously at the station from a very low altitude. Thence he continued his descent into the marsh. On alighting he saw the one unexploded bomb, and set fire to his machine, knowing that the bomb would ensure its destruction. He then proceeded towards Turkish territory.

At this moment he perceived Squadron-Commander Davies descending, and fearing that he would come down near the burning machine and thus risk destruction from the bomb, Flight Sub-Lieutenant Smylie ran back, and from a shots distance exploded the bomb by means of a pistol bullet. Squadron-Commander Davies descended at a safe distance from the burning machine, took up Sub-Lieutenant Smylie, in spite of the near approach of a party of the enemy, and returned to the aerodrome.

The terse, official *Gazette* so far commits itself as to comment, in conclusion:

"A feat of airmanship that can seldom have been equalled for skill and gallantry."

Hawker—Major Lane George, D.S.O., R.E., and R.F.C.—was one of the earlier "stars." Crossing to France with the original R.F.C. squadron, attached to the B.E.F., in September 1914, he took aeroplane pilot's "ticket" 435, at Hendon, on a Deperdussin monoplane, March 4th, 1913. For tackling eleven Boche machines, single-handed, in 1915, he was awarded the D.S.O.; and for "most conspicuous bravery and very great ability" on July 25th, 1915, the Victoria Cross.

When flying alone he attacked three German aeroplanes in succession. The first managed eventually to escape, the second was driven to the ground damaged, and the third, which he attacked at a height of about 10,000 feet, was driven to earth in our lines, the pilot and observer being killed.

He was shot down and killed by the notorious von Richthofen.

Another British airman with whom this German "ace "fought a savage duel—lasting almost sixty minutes, at a height of over 10,000 feet—was Second-Lieutenant Gilbert Insall, V.C. At the critical moment both men ran out of ammunition. After gaily waving his hand, the "Red Battle Flyer" disappeared behind the clouds, and Insall returned to his base. A few weeks later he "put up" the following great "stunt":

Patrolling in a Vickers fighting machine, with First-class Air Mechanic T. H. Donald as gunner, a German machine was sighted, pursued, and attacked near Achiet. The German pilot led the Vickers machine over a rocket battery, but with great skill Lieutenant Insall dived, and got to close range, when Donald fired a drum of cartridges into the German machine, stopping its engine.

The German pilot then dived through a cloud, followed by Lieutenant Insall. Fire was again opened, and the German machine was brought down heavily in a ploughed field four miles south-east of Arras. On seeing the Germans scramble out of their machine and prepare to fire, Lieutenant Insall dived to 500 feet, thus enabling Donald to open heavy fire on them. The Germans then fled, one helping the other, who was apparently wounded. Other Germans then commenced heavy fire, but in spite of this Lieutenant Insall turned again, and an incendiary bomb was dropped on the German machine, which was last seen wreathed in smoke.

Lieutenant Insall then headed west in order to get back over the German trenches, but as he was at only 2,000 feet altitude, he dived across them for greater speed, Donald firing into the trenches as he passed over. The German fire, however, damaged the petrol tank, and, with great coolness, Lieutenant Insall landed under cover of a wood 500 yards inside our lines. The Germans fired some 150 shells at our machine on the ground, but without causing material damage. Much damage had, however, been caused by rifle fire, but during the night it was repaired behind screened lights, and at dawn Lieutenant Insall flew his machine home with First-class Air Mechanic T. H. Donald as a passenger.

Before returning home for his investiture, Insall determined upon a last farewell flight over the Hun lines. Unfortunately, he encountered there a revengeful member of the Richthofen Chasing Squadron, was brought down, and taken prisoner.

(*Vide Richthofen & Böelcke in Their Own Words* by Manfred Freiherr von Richthofen & Oswald Böelcke: Leonaur 2011.)

This, however, was far from the last to be heard of this extraordinarily versatile young man. After twenty months in solitary confinement at Cologne, he succeeded in breaking out of his prison; made his way across Germany, and *via* Holland, to England, where he was subsequently decorated by George V., who had a long talk with him regarding his experiences.

Insall was peculiarly the type of young man who haunts racing-tracks and aerodromes: the monosyllabic youth of muscular frame, with steel wrists, unflickering grey eyes—behind which lie such a wealth of meaning and emotions that so rarely find voice; a sunny, cheerful temperament that makes light of hardship and adversity; and an idiosyncrasy of dress—hair brushed back well from the forehead, hat invariably worn at a rakish angle, clothes spotted with petrol and smelling strongly of oil—and manner which rides calmly all ridicule and criticism. A type that is ever frightened, but never afraid!

However, that is only one type attracted to aviation. On close observation one will notice that personality predominates among our crack pilots, from Warneford, reckless to a degree and possessed of a warm imagination, to Rhodes-Moorhouse, who in the whole of his twenty-five years never let a word pass his lips concerning his own attainments, and was accredited by his friends as "fearing nothing on heaven or earth," and to John Aidan Liddell.

Had you been acquainted with the latter, you would have accredited him studious—a shy, somewhat bashful youth. An elusive personality that charmed with the very simplicity of its nature, the beauty of its ideal, the breadth of its knowledge and interest in life, a potential scientist, or a brilliant leader of research, was Liddell—in reality one of life's greatest heroes, who, before he died, left on record a deed unequalled even in our glorious records.

> When on a flying reconnaissance over Ostend-Bruges-Ghent he was severely wounded (his right thigh being broken), which caused momentary unconsciousness, but by a great effort he recovered partial control after his machine had dropped nearly 3,000 feet, and, notwithstanding his collapsed state, succeeded, although continually fired at, in completing his course, and brought the aeroplane into our lines half an hour after he had been wounded, (thus saving the life of his observer.)

On the latter all his thoughts were concentrated. As he lay upon his sick-bed, with the knowledge that the grim hand of Death was hourly creeping nearer, Aidan Liddell wrote to his mother in England:

> Mummy Dear,
> Don't be alarmed at my little escapade; will be all right again soon and be with you. . . . Poor Peck (his observer), what an awful time he must have had after I fainted and we were nose-diving headlong for the ground. . . . The major told me today that I have been recommended for the V.C. . . .
> P.S. —Please don't go talking about this business to all the old dowagers of your acquaintance.

Seven days later he was dead.

The V.C. exploit of Second-Lieutenant Rhodes-Moorhouse was a similar affair—the temperament of the two men as dissimilar as possible. In those wonder pre-war days of 1913-14 at "Brooklands,"

"R.M." and his little two-seater racing-car were most familiar figures, one might almost venture to say, institutions. With a flash, a rattle, and a whiff of petrol the two would whiz past one in a narrow country road; missing other vehicles by inches, and turning corners on a most amazing equipoise of the two near-side rims.

The modesty, charm, and unselfishness of the man were, item and item, the sum of his friendship. His skill and daring were bywords around the racing-track. His courage and fortitude were yet to be revealed. When the curtain of the world-war drama rolled back and the stage of battle was revealed in all its pitiless detail, the story of Rhodes-Moorhouse's V.C. was of those few incidents which lent the affair that atmosphere of knightliness and chivalry which distinguished the battlefield of mediaeval times. Here it is:

> For most conspicuous bravery on April 26th, 1915, in flying to Courtrai and dropping bombs on the railway-line near that station. On starting the return journey, he was mortally wounded, but succeeded in flying for thirty-five miles to his destination, and reported the successful accomplishment of his object. He died of his wounds.

The deeds of McNamara, Read, Rees, Robinson, and Warneford, in order told, make the sum complete.

McNamara, lieutenant in the Australian Forces, attached to the R.F.C., was participating in:

> An aerial bomb attack upon a hostile construction train, when one of our pilots was forced to land behind the enemy's lines. Observing this pilot's predicament, and the fact that hostile cavalry were approaching, he immediately descended to his rescue. He did his best under heavy rifle fire, and in spite of the fact that he himself had been severely wounded in the thigh. He landed about 200 yards from the damaged machine, the pilot of which climbed on to Lieutenant McNamara's machine, and an attempt was made to rise.
>
> Owing, however, to his disabled leg, Lieutenant McNamara was unable to keep his machine straight, and it turned over. The two officers, having extricated themselves, immediately set fire to the machine, and made their way across to the damaged machine, which they succeeded in starting. Finally, Lieutenant McNamara, although weak from loss of blood, flew this machine back to the aerodrome, a distance of seventy miles, and

thus completed his comrade's rescue.

Captain Anketall Montray Read was awarded his Gross, before transferring to the Flying Corps, for a gallant piece of work at Hillock, that included carrying "out of action an officer who was mortally wounded, under a hot fire from rifles and grenades."

> Whilst on flying duties, Major Rees sighted what he thought to be a bombing party of our own machines returning home. He went up to escort them, but on getting nearer discovered they were a party of enemy machines, about ten in all. Major Rees was immediately attacked by one of the machines, and after a short encounter it disappeared behind the enemy lines, damaged. Five others then attacked him at long range, but these he dispersed on coming to close quarters, after seriously damaging two of the machines.
>
> Seeing two others going westwards, he gave chase to them, but on coming nearer he was wounded in the thigh, causing him to lose temporary control of his machine He soon righted it, and immediately closed with the enemy, firing at a close-contact range of only a few yards, until all his ammunition was used up. He then returned home, landing his machine safely in our lines.

Leefe Robinson won the V.C. and worldwide renown at Cuffley for bringing down a raiding Zeppelin, for the first time on these shores.

> He attacked an enemy airship under circumstances of great difficulty and danger, and sent it crashing to the ground as a flaming wreck. He had been in the air for more than two hours, and had previously attacked another airship during his flight.

And Flight-Sub-Lieutenant Warneford's was the first of the Naval "blue ribbons," conferred upon him in the record space of twenty-four hours, for bringing down a Zepp. near Evere, on June 7th, 1915.

CHAPTER 8

Watchers of the Skies

It is difficult to connect the statement that a "successful raid was carried out last night by Canadian troops at Lens" with the elongated, unlovely form of the kite-balloons, floating gently in the morning breeze, five or six miles behind the lines. Like the eyes of a giant octopus, they stud the grey warfront at regular intervals, from the sea to the dim indistinction of the south horizon. Stolid, almost immobile in appearance, there are alert eyes peering earthward from that tiny basket beneath the green gas-bag that are restless and without avoidance.

Enemy arrivals and departures, even to the hour of his—or at the time he should be having his morning "tub," and the movement of road and railway traffic to his various headquarters, have been reduced by lengthened observation to a schedule, as reliable as a railway timetable. At—shall we say—eleven every morning, a supply train comes puffing down that stretch of shell-pocked country from L—— to M——, halting at M——. At three in the afternoon, it returns. At an hour after sunrise and an hour before sunset a particular group of heavy guns shell the little town of P—— behind the British lines with unfailing regularity.

Should the train be delayed up country, and late on her time; should that bombardment vary but a few moments: within sixty seconds the information is in the hands—or rather the ears—of the intelligence officer responsible. A battalion or a company coming up for relief, a new gun opening fire, digging begun on a new series of emplacements—these aerial detectives will have the details immediately at their finger ends.

Riding steadily from the first bright hour of the morning to the fading visibility of the twilight, the observer, with the enemy lines spread out before him, a living replica of the large-scale map in his balloon, in direct communication with the British "heavies" and with other balloons, amasses a maze of details and accurate information that the aeroplane, at a high altitude and travelling at a tremendous speed, may overlook. Hours may pass, but finally, as inevitable as fate, the reward will come.

The red flash of a battery shows up at some unexpected point in the green-grey panorama. A second later the telephone-bell by the ground-winch will ring:

New Boche battery observed at A8,A4.6. Put me through to the 'nine-point-two' at M——.

The ensuing official conversation between the observer, swaying 1,000 feet or more above the earth, and the artillery captain alongside his gun, hidden in a tiny wood two miles away across country, we may not overhear. But we can see the gun's crew tumbling out of billets. Off comes the tarpaulin—like the cloth from a table. An ominous-looking shell is brought up, by hand, from some mysterious recess and rammed home. The men stand by.

Then the telephone in the balloon starts up. It is the battery speaking. "We are going to open fire"—nothing more! That shot, however, may be the prelude to a great advance; on the other hand, the first signal for an extended defensive barrage. The observer keeps the speaking-tube to his mouth, and watches. His eyes are glued to that tiny half square mile of surface before him. Somewhere below, there echoes the dull boom of heavy artillery. A distant screaming fills the air. Somewhere ahead there is a sudden burst of flame and smoke.

His comment to the battery commander is terse and to the point: "Over!" Again, the operation is repeated. This time the monosyllabic advice varies to: "Short!" Then a few seconds later an eager whisper: "Target!" From now on, we may say, the balloonist is only a spectator. The dull boom of the gun comes floating up, with methodical regularity. The burst is, if anything, rather more methodical in its vicinity. The observer may enjoy a well-earned rest!

Then, sweeping across the sky-line, comes the sinister grey form of H.A.—hostile aircraft. Anti-aircraft guns open on all sides. Immediately below a machine gun commences to rattle and bark. Taking advantage of a rolling bank of low-lying clouds, the daring enemy aviator is diving for the balloon with a murderous directness. Emerging from the toe of the cloud, he is almost in line with the head of the K.B. A bomb drops, and another—harmless enough. The fourth, however, strikes the gas-bag at a glancing angle. A column of heavy black smoke belches skywards. Two tiny black specks descend rapidly from the basket. The crew have taken to their parachutes—the life-boats of the sinking ship. After an unpleasant and trying five minutes they land, little worse for their adventure.

Tomorrow a fresh balloon will have taken its place. A similar Hun craft, possibly more, will have paid the revenge. Tomorrow the same observer in the same position will be informing the same battery that "his last shot went over." The Hun aeroplane will come winging across the clouds, possibly with the same success, more probably to pay the penalty of his daring. The air-war is one of incessant give and take—give and take!

Conditions will have changed; the defence blossomed into an offensive. Working in co-operation with other craft and his batteries, the observer will now be making suggestions for the locality of the barrage. Shot by shot, some will record the artillery fire. Others will be guaranteeing the effectiveness of the demolition behind the enemy's lines. A reinforcement of balloons will have been rushed up overnight—in the darkness—and concentrated as secretly as possible in masked camps.

At the dawn they will startle the quiet countryside, floating up heavenward from behind all manner of unsuspected declivities and woods—an endless cordon, as far as eye can reach. All the morning, and far on into the afternoon, they will be directing artillery fire, without cessation. Then with nightfall, the Canadians—or, whatever troops they may be, will go scrambling over the top, into the adventurous shadows of "No Man's Land," and on into the Boche trenches.

That is the modern warfare combination of sky and earth.

CHAPTER 9

The Navy That Flies

(Per adua, ad astra)

On July 1st, 1914, the R.N.A.S. —formerly Naval Wing of the
Royal Flying Corps—came into being as a separate unit of the Im-
perial Forces. The Force was commanded by Commodore Sueter,
M.V.O., R.N., who had under him one Commander—Samson,
D.S.O. —some half a dozen squadron commanders, who ranked as
Lieutenant-Commanders R.N., and a personnel of 700 officers and
men. The command was composed of one large base for land ma-
chines, with five smaller stations for sea-planes along the coast.

It was not long before the new service had an opportunity of
showing its worth, for the fleet, assembled for a great test mobilisation—which eventuated in a mobilisation for war—was to be inspect-
ed by the king, and the seaplanes intended giving a display with an
aggregate force of sixty-two, twenty moored with the fleet, one flying
boat, and some score of aeroplanes. Affairs of State prevented the king
from being present at the review, but the seaplane programme was
carried out in its entirety.

Immediately afterwards war was declared, and the new service, with
its handful of antediluvian craft, by dawn of August 5th, 1914, were
busy patrolling the coasts and the North Sea for German aircraft and
submarines, and convoying troopships of the British Expeditionary
Force to the scene of war. Of these craft no single machine had a British engine. The horse-power, ranging from 100 to 160, was supplied
by both water and air-cooled engines, and there had been no attempt
at standardisation.

Of other types of aircraft, the R.N.A.S. possessed a score or so
of spherical balloons—employed for observational purposes and the
direction of artillery—some British "Baby" airships, which had been
handed over by the army a month or so previous, and a small but use-

ful German airship.

Thus equipped, the naval arm undertook not only Home Defence, but supplied a squadron for patrol work along the Belgian coast. The naval aircraft, by a series of daring raids, attacked effectively enemy destroyers in the North Sea, and destroyed submarines, harbour-works, ammunition-dumps, road and railway transport, billets, and aerodromes in Belgium, thus forming a sound line of defence against the enemy's vaunted ambition, to invade the shores of England.

To the time when the Royal Naval Air Service with the Royal Flying Corps was merged into the Royal Air Force, the British Naval Air Service has been incessantly at work, its activities extending from the British Isles to wherever the British naval and military forces have operated.

The early work of the service was marked by the 1914 Christmas Day raid on Cuxhaven; the attacks on Zeppelin sheds at Düsseldorf and Friedrichshaven; the intrepid flying in Mesopotamia and the dropping of 19,500 lbs. of food and a quantity of medical stores into Kut between April 15th and April 29th, 1916; the operations in the Eastern Mediterranean, where throughout the Peninsular campaign the Royal Naval Air Service flew for both army and navy; in East Africa and Rufigi, including the "spotting" and bombing of the German warship *Koenigsberg*; the combating of enemy airmen on their way to or returning from raiding this country; the destruction of three Zeppelins by Royal Naval aircraft; in addition to the work as "eyes of the fleet" in the vigil kept by our surface craft in the North Sea, the Mediterranean, and elsewhere.

One of the earliest operations in the Battle of Jutland Bank was the sending up of a seaplane by Sir David Beatty to identify four enemy cruisers, the seaplanes having to fly at a height of goo feet within 3,000 yards in order to accomplish their purpose.

During the operations against the German Battle Cruiser Squadron which appeared off the East Coast on the morning of April 25th, 1916, two Zeppelins were pursued by a seaplane, and three submarines were forced to submerge by another machine, while other airmen, in spite of heavy anti-aircraft fire, dropped bombs on the retiring cruisers.

The larger part of the effort of the "home" sections of the Royal Naval Air Service during the last fifteen months has consisted in "operations in the vicinity of the coast."

In the early stages of the war the Royal Naval Air Service also provided crews for armoured cars which operated against the Germans in Belgium, while armoured-car operations have been carried out against the Austrians, Bulgarians, and Turks.

The concerted attacks on this country in 1915 by Zeppelins gave the Royal Naval Air Service plenty of scope. Flight-Lieutenant Warneford gained his V.C. by bringing down a Zeppelin near Ghent on June 7th of that year; and on August 9th naval aircraft attacked a returning Zeppelin and destroyed it. In all, three Zeppelins have been accounted for. In combating German aeroplanes on their way to or returning from raids on London and other places in this country, the service has been most successful. In twenty-four raids, twenty-two enemy machine were rendered *hors de combat* and two others were reported to have shared a similar fate.

The submarine-catching activity has extended to bases in the Mediterranean, where both seaplanes, airships, and seaplane-carriers are employed. And naval aeroplanes have co-operated with the army in the north of France, in Salonica, Italy, Mesopotamia, Palestine, Egypt, and British East Africa.

Where the development of the Military Wing has been with personnel, that of the R.N.A.S. has been with aircraft. It must be remembered, where the former employed only aeroplanes—the military kite-balloon not making its appearance until the end of 1915—the latter has been responsible for both land machine, seaplane, seaplane-carrier, balloon, kite-balloon, and airship.

As Sir Eric Geddes stated recently in the House of Commons:

The personnel of 700 had increased to 41,000. . . . The duties were varied, of great value and of absorbing interest.

Naval airships and seaplanes are the terror of the enemy submarine. During a single month the aircraft patrol round the British coast alone is more than five times the circumference of the earth. During the month of September 1917 sixty-four raids were carried out on dockyards, naval depots, aerodromes, and other objects of military importance in Flanders beyond the enemy lines. No fewer than 2,736 bombs were dropped by the R.N.A.S., totalling eighty-five tons of explosives.

He added:

There is no doubt, that these raids result in great material and moral damage, and on many occasions their effect is shown in the aerial photographs to be such as to hamper and restrict seriously the enemy naval, military, and aerial undertakings.

The service is commanded by a commodore of the first class, automatically a member of the Board of Admiralty. Two other commodores are under him, with more than half a dozen post-captains, wing-commanders by the dozen, and squadron-commanders innumerable.

The R.N.A.S. now issues an almost daily communique of its doings, and has stations all along the coast, many of them with more machines than the entire service possessed at the outbreak of war, and is busily engaged in convoying food-ships in dangerous waters.

As an instance of a fortnight's work by four of these naval squadrons with the Royal Flying Corps, the following details will give some idea of the work carried out. Over 250 machines were attacked, twenty-six were brought down, over thirty were driven down, while some 150 offensive patrol raids were made, in addition to supplying escorting machines and carrying out reconnaissances. "Spotting" for the heavy artillery has been frequently undertaken on the Western Front, and commendation has been bestowed on the squadrons and kite-balloon sections of the Royal Naval Air Service.

The work of the Royal Naval Air Service in bombing Zeebrugge, the docks at Ostend, German bases and aerodromes in Belgium and France, has been constant—hardly a fortnight has gone by without a series of such raids—while repeated attacks on destroyers, torpedo-boats, drifters, and minesweepers have been undertaken.

On August 9th, 1917, was the successful raid on the Zeppelin sheds near Brussels. On August 25th a successful attack was made on Zeppelin sheds at Cogneloe, near Namur. On April 23rd, 1918, three British machines attacked five enemy destroyers between Blankenburg and Zeebrugge, and a direct hit was made on the leading vessel which took a list to port; only four of the destroyers were seen to enter Zeebrugge harbour, and it was thought probable that the bombed vessel was sunk. The following morning vessels in Zeebrugge harbour were bombed, and a day later an air attack was made on four destroyers discovered at sea north of Ostend.

Towards the close of the last summer two flights of five Sopwith scouts encountered approximately twenty-five hostile machines between Ostend and Ghistelles, and a general engagement took place. Our machines completely broke up the enemy formation, and a number of hostile machines were either destroyed or badly damaged.

Engaging three hostile machines consecutively, one British airman shot two down completely out of control, and a third possibly; and five others were accounted for. There were several other combats, but none of these could be considered decisive. All our machines returned safely, although five of them were badly shot about, one machine having no less than 113 bullet-holes and both petrol-tanks pierced.

Throughout the whole of the operations in the Dardanelles Peninsula the air operations were undertaken by the Royal Naval Air Service for both land and naval services. Reconnaissance work was frequently done, some valuable photographic information was obtained, while on a number of occasions the Royal Naval Air Service successfully interfered with the railway and road transport. The Berlin-Constantinople line, largely used for transport of war material, has been frequently bombed, forage stores and munition dumps being fired, and bridges badly damaged in spite of active hostile gunfire; while trains in motion have been bombed and attacked with machine guns. The Zeitumlik Powder Factory at Constantinople was bombed, and frequent visits were made to Adrianople station, involving long flights, in some cases of over 400 miles.

Crop-burning was another operation performed by the Royal Naval Air Service, enormous damage being inflicted with incendiary bombs. Attacks on enemy battleships, destroyers, and transports in the Dardanelles were frequent, and, to quote the Turkish report, in one case only, one battleship "arrived at Constantinople with her centre turret damaged and ten men killed as the result of an aeroplane bomb." A number of flights have had to be made over the open sea on aeroplanes unprovided with floats.

One of the longest night flights in the early stages of the war was that undertaken from a station in the Dardanelles area for the purpose of attacking a railway bridge at Kuleli Burgaz. The airman on his flight to the objective was subjected to heavy anti-aircraft fire. He descended to within 300 feet of the bridge before releasing his bombs, both of which apparently hit the bridge. Just afterwards engine trouble developed, and it was with difficulty that the airman returned to his station.

Particular attention was paid on one occasion to Chanak, in consequence of information that the Kaiser and his entourage was paying a visit. Everything pointed to arrangements being made for something spectacular for the Supreme War Lord, and abnormal activity on the part of the enemy in the Dardanelles, together with elaborate precautions for reporting movements of British aircraft, all tended to confirm the genuineness of the reported visit. In spite of very unfavourable weather, the operation, which it was realised would be attended by considerable risk, was carried out; several machines set out, but only one succeeded in reaching the objective. This airman dropped a number of bombs on the town.

On his return journey he struck the side of a mountain in the darkness and the machine caught fire on crashing. The pilot, although severely injured, was able to climb out of his machine, and was found next morning by a Greek shepherd. At dawn next day, in extremely bad weather, seven machines effectively bombed the town, in spite of heavy anti-aircraft fire.

The first Gotha squad to take part in the war operated in Salonica. A steady offensive in Southern Bulgaria by the Royal Naval Air Service had a most demoralising effect on the enemy. For some time, places where the heaviest anti-aircraft fire was encountered were singled out for special attention, and after several visits our machines were able to fly over these places with little or no opposition.

It was mainly due to the efforts of the British Armoured Car Division that the enemy did not break the line in the fighting with the Russians in the Dobrudja early in December 1916, and the commander received an autograph letter from the general commanding the 4th Siberian Army, thanking the officers and men for their brave and unselfish work;

In October 1916 a number of Royal Naval Air Service machines were despatched from Imbros to Bucharest, a distance of 310 miles. All the machines arrived, after great difficulty, owing to thunderstorms and thick mists. One machine, after passing westward of Adrianople, experienced bad weather in the Balkan Mountains, and owing to a thunderstorm the pilot lost control. He fell from 9,000 feet to 1,000 feet, at which height he emerged from the cloud upside-down, regaining control at 500 feet.

While in the cloud the machine looped the loop several times, and the compass became useless. He landed to repair his machine on a spot which was close to a Bulgarian camp. As he was taxiing off, a party of Bulgarians opened fire, and charging them, the pilot scattered them with a few rounds from his machine gun. While he was following the course of a river in the hope of striking the Danube, about thirty Bulgarians on a barge opened fire with rifles. Returning, the pilot emptied a tray of ammunition into them, causing them all to jump into the water. After crossing the Danube, he ran into rain and fog, completely losing his bearings, and ultimately coming down in Russian territory, whence he returned to Bucharest by train.

In the Egypt and Palestine operations valuable reconnaissances were made. El Arish, Horns, Beirut, Bursir, Haifa, the Levisi district were bombed and large fires caused. A very destructive raid was carried out by ten seaplanes up the Haifa-Afuleh Valley. Besides considerably damaging the camp, a train proceeding south was bombed and damaged, the permanent way was broken up in various places, and a railway engine, fourteen carriages, and a large amount of stores burnt.

The whole operation was carried out against strong anti-aircraft fire, and although each one of our machines was hit, all returned safely. In the bombing of Horns station, a flight of forty-five miles inland, in a strong wind, causing heavy weather, and crossing hills 1,800 feet high in clouds at 1,500 feet, a seaplane of a heavier type made an exceptionally fine flight.

The East African aeroplane squadron cooperating with General van Deventer's column carried out reconnaissances ahead of the Army and bombed the German encampments. The country in which the squadron operated in one section of the campaign made it impossible to land a machine without wrecking it, except in aerodromes and sometimes in river-beds. Much useful work was done in map-making over a difficult country; while the enemy's porter transport was considerably harassed, and despatches were carried when other means of communication between the distant columns had failed. On several occasions the G.O.C. was taken up in a machine for observation purposes.

CHAPTER 10

From Shore to Shore

From dawn to sundown; from the toe of Cornwall's rugged cliffs to the bleak shores of the Shetland Islands; from the grey rock of Gibraltar, standing sentinel to the western gate of the Mediterranean, to its counterpart at sun-baked Suez; from Dunmore Head, in the extreme south, to Belfast Lough, in the extreme north of Ireland; from Harwich, across the cold grey wastes of the North Sea, to Borkum, with a blue sky o'erhead and a favourable tide, you may see the British Naval Air Service (Royal Air Force) at work; hugging the shore, or far out hovering over the sea, like giant seagulls dipping down for their prey. The craft vary from slim grey airships to kite-balloons rising ungainly from the belly of a ship and giant Curtiss flying boats. But their quest is ever the same—the nefarious Hun U-boat.

Here Jules Verne's monsters of the underseas and Wells's aerial avengers meet in grim and incessant death-conflict. Here the most up-to-date inventions of modern science are slowly but surely deciding the grave issue of Civilisation versus Barbarity. A shattered periscope in a pool of floating oil, an aerial bird that lies broken and helpless at the water's edge, may seem but small marks in this whirlpool of Armageddon; yet each in their turn marks a long step forward in the march. The methods they employ? You may gauge those best from the anecdotes of battle which follow on.

Scouring the sky, Seaplane X. sighted a large convoy, ten miles distant; between them an enemy submarine, fully on the surface, travelling at a low speed, and within two miles of the convoy. Winging her way, "full-out," at ninety miles an hour, at the same time diving and preparing to attack, she made for the U-boat. The latter did not sight her until she was only three miles distant. Then, at once, she commenced to submerge. When the seaplane reached bombing position, the top of the conning-tower was just awash, and both periscopes were out

Two large bombs were released, the first of which exploded directly on the conning-tower, and the periscopes were seen to collapse. The second bomb hit the water thirty feet ahead of the conning-tower in a direct line with the fore end of the submarine. The seaplane then turned and observed a considerable disturbance on the surface of the water, with quantities of air rushing up, giving the appearance of boiling. Two other bombs were dropped from a thousand feet, one of which exploded in the midst of the disturbance.

In addition to the discoloration of the water caused by the bombs, brown and white matter was observed to rise to the surface. The seaplane remained over the spot for a few minutes, during which the disturbance continued, slightly increasing in intensity. The submarine appeared to be of a large type, painted black, carrying two guns, one forward and one aft of the conning-tower.

How a British seaplane of a larger type succeeded in sinking a U-boat, in face of the united attack of three other submarines, three destroyers, and two seaplanes escorting them, is an epic of Air Service history. Here is the making on't. One misty morning the seaplane sighted the submarine in near vicinity. The latter was painted light grey, with a mast and a gun, on what appeared to be a raised deck. By the gun was one of the crew. Flying directly over the enemy, the aircraft dropped a bomb, hitting the tail of the underseas craft direct. As she turned to repeat the attack, the British airmen observed that the explosion had made a large rent in the deck, and photographed it. Then, patches of red and grey shell-burst unexpectedly bit into the grey shroud of the mist, heralding the approach of the enemy reinforcements.

All six vessels opened fire on our machine, but none of their shells was effective. The enemy seaplanes were unable to approach, owing to the barrage put up by the destroyers. As our seaplane again turned completely round and passed over the submarine, which by this time was sinking by the stern, water being up to the conning-tower and the nose full out of the water, a second bomb was released, exploding fifteen feet ahead of the bow of the submarine, causing it to vibrate and sink immediately. The sea-surface stained with a quantity of blackish oil, air-bubbles, and strange matter. The destroyers and other submarines closed in on the British seaplane, which, having no further bombs, had to be content with sparking a wireless message to her base, stating the position of the destroyers, and returning home in safety.

Hunting in couples, a brace of seaplanes sighted an enemy submarine fully blown, travelling about fourteen knots, and at once dived to the attack. Two men were on the conning-tower at the time. The first machine to reach her dropped a bomb which found good target, being detonated on the starboard side of the submarine, halfway between the stern and the conning-tower.

The submarine heeled slowly over to port and remained in that position, stopped in her own length and began to sink stern first, the bow rising high above the water. The second machine dropped a bomb just as the conning-tower was disappearing. It exploded in front, on the port side. After this bomb had detonated, a further explosion occurred under water, apparently at the bow of the submarine, followed by several smaller explosions. Other bombs were dropped. The two men were still on the conning-tower as the vessel sank, but nothing further was seen of them, although the area was searched for fifteen minutes. No oil or wreckage was seen.

Another instance was that of a seaplane which swooped down 4,000 feet out of the skies, and obtained two direct hits on a trailing submarine. Flying in consort with two aeroplanes, on patrol, she had sighted this enemy craft—one of an unusually large type, with two periscopes—from a distance. Both bombs fell abaft the conning-tower, one, at least, a palpably direct hit. Suddenly the submarine plunged over on her back, and with a last tremendous wriggle, vomiting quantities of oil, disappeared. The lean periscope knifing the surface of the water, the sudden, roaring downwards sweep of wings, the chaos of the explosion, the tell-tale patch of oil on the water's edge—the incidents vary little in the main details, the craft occasionally.

Opinion in aviation circles is sharply divided as to the merits and the demerits of their respective craft, the lighter- and the heavier-than-air. An airship man will tell you—and not in the strictest confidence—that an aeroplane, or, for that matter, a seaplane is "a rakish, good-for-nothing bus." The invariable retort of the heavier-than-air pilot is that "an airship is a 'gas-bag,' harmless and helpless." May be that is correct. But they have ample evidence in their defence. Their normal flying altitude is invaluable for this class of work. Neither too high nor too low, from this height the bed of the sea to a depth of twenty fathoms is plainly distinguishable. The sinister black form worming its way against the sandy colour of the bottom, within the fathom limit, stands in dire peril from above. For where the airman can see distinctly, the submerged submarine commander is blind! When, eventually, he comes to the surface, he will find his deadly enemy awaiting him.

In one instance, an airship pilot patrolling about noontime sighted a suspicious patch of oil on the surface of the water. Rapidly he sank lower, to investigate—and watch. For his trouble he was rewarded, ten minutes later, with the sight of a periscope breaking water—to immediately disappear. However, swift as she was, a bomb found the swirl of her descent.

When the maelstrom of the explosion died away, oil and bubbles in large quantities came rippling to the surface. Below, the submarine was to be seen creeping slowly along, with an unhealthy list to port. The airship pilot made play with more bombs. More bubbles and air rose to the surface, also two heavy swirls. Meanwhile a trawler and two motor-craft, which had watched from afar, came dashing to the scene of fray. Several depth-charges were brought into action, and more bombs were dropped; and the surface craft kept watch till after sunset. But nothing further was seen or heard of that submarine.

To witness a submarine attack on a helpless merchantman was the ill—or rather good fortune of another airship pilot. He flew down on the wind, at full speed, to the spot. The submarine saw him coming and submerged. Undaunted, he dropped two bombs directly on the spot whence she had disappeared. In a short time, several large bubbles—one in particular being of huge size—came to the surface. This disturbance of the water continued for five minutes. Two trawlers which had come up dropped depth-charges immediately; three of which exploded right over the target. More oil came up. And just at this juncture the wind, which had been blowing at great force, increased to a gale, and several fitments of the airship being carried away, she returned to the base.

Patrolling one November afternoon, another seaplane discovered a submarine in the act of diving and a second submarine stationary on the surface. Spiralling down, the pilot got directly over the stationary submarine and two bombs were loosed, one of which hit the decks fairly amidships. The submarine was hidden by the smoke of the bomb, and when that cleared away, the vessel was sinking with both ends in the air. In a few minutes the submarine had disappeared, and again a large quantity of oil came to the surface. Nothing further was seen of the first submarine.

More often than not, unfortunately, the underseas craft is successful in its quest. But sometimes the little God of Chance, perched, grimly sardonic, among the clouds, will send an avenging plane speeding down at the identical—and most unfortunate—moment. Flying out to meet a merchant ship, a pilot observed a large disturbance on the water, 200 yards away from the vessel. Just afterwards the wake of a torpedo was seen, but it missed the ship by a few yards. The seaplane at once planed down, and in less than a minute after sighting the submarine's movements dropped two bombs which fell and exploded within eight yards of each other. Large quantities of oil and bubbles then rose to the surface, while the merchantman proceeded on her course in safety.

Two other large seaplanes, while on patrol, sighted an enemy submarine on the surface. The first seaplane dropped a bomb which exploded just abaft the centre of the submarine. The submarine listed heavily to port and went down by the stern within one minute. The second seaplane passed over the enemy just as he sank and dropped a bomb which exploded in the centre of the swirl caused by the submarine's disappearance. Two further bombs were dropped, and nothing more was seen of the submarine.

These air-pilots never miss an opportunity. A seaplane saw a submarine come to the surface. The pilot flashed across it in a headlong dive, dropped a bomb, overshot his target, and turned in immediately to the attack again, to see the submarine disappearing with a list of thirty degrees to port. He dropped a second bomb where she had disappeared, and a few minutes later a patch of oil about 150 feet long and twelve feet wide appeared on the surface. That submarine hunts no more.

Chapter 11

An Aerial Push

The commanding officer of X. Squadron sat at his small office table. Before him lay compasses, pencil, and scale-map, the latter of the district that lay fifteen miles on either side of the firing-lines. Marked off neatly into ruled squares, the canvas contour was printed here and there with odd letters, the larger squares imaginarily subdivided from one to ten. Thus, at a single glance he could locate either town or village, railway junction or ammunition dump, to the fraction of a yard. The commanding officer thought tensely.

He studied the coloured surface steadily, moving his compasses from side to side and jotting down certain figures on a stray sheet as he went. This task completed to his satisfaction, he drew some buff official documents from his pocket and read them through with care. Then his reconnaissance pilot came in.

Together they discussed the official report, with due comment on the part of the senior officer, whose concluding remark was curt and very much to the point. "As I figure it out," he said, "the enemy is intending establishing a large ammunition dump at this position"—he indicated a point on the map—"probably for a concentration of artillery in this sector, possibly as the prelude to an infantry attack on a large scale. That dump must be destroyed at all costs."

The pilot saluted smartly and went out; An hour later he presented a detailed account. Read in the terse phraseology of report form it ran: "10,000 feet, 10.20 a.m. B,D2.5. Observed congestion traffic on the roads and railways. Former lined to length of half a mile with convoy of ammunition motor-lorries—convoy proceeding westerly direction. On the sidings of the railway-track, which lies approximately half a mile due east of this point—B,Dz.5 two long trains of trucks—approximate number twelve apiece—both heading west. In S—— station, half-mile to the east, another train observed; locomotive with steam up, heading same direction.

Distinct evidences of some form of building taking place in a small wood that runs alongside the main road—B,D2.4. Surface of surrounding fields marked with distinct traces newly-worn footpaths; all leading up to the point B,D 2.5. Significant fact that, though in this sector anti-aircraft bombardment usually severe, today I was able to circle round at a low altitude without a shot being fired."

On the strength of this, the C.O. despatched a photographic machine to the map position B,D2.5. The latter pilot's mission was no sinecure. Flying extremely low—to acquire better focus—they will be working through an incessant anti-aircraft bombardment for an hour or an hour and a half on end. Within an hour of landing their new negatives will have been developed. Thence they are passed on to the Intelligence Department, who compare them with previous photos of the same area.

This case proved no exception to the rule. Headquarters tested it, first by this theory, and then by that; discussed it; deprecated it; and finally— Whether the fact that, late that night, two large transports slipped down Southampton Water into the inky darkness of the Channel, with, battened securely beneath their hatches, the accumulated portions of several heavy-calibre howitzers, and the 2nd E——s and the 14th W——s received sudden marching orders, where they were quartered in a sleepy village in the south of England, that their services to their king and country would be of more value elsewhere—that elsewhere being vaguely intimated to be somewhere in the north of France—has any connection, may best be judged from ensuing events.

Anyhow, for the members of X—— squadron the following week was one of the busiest of their embittered young lives. Every pilot had his hands full; reconnaissance, bombing, and combat bound. The observers went with them. And every branch of work was a specialised branch.

In fact, every pilot and observer in the Flying Corps today is employed with some special purpose, the craft included, and they vary from the fast rapid-climbing fighting machines to the slower and more cumbrous reconnaissance and spotting craft with greater powers of duration. There are varying degrees of pilots, and the observers have varying degrees of duty to perform. But every available aeroplane was necessary to X—— squadron for the particular job they had on hand.

Primarily it was necessary to gain undisputed sway of their particular section of the aerial front. This was accomplished by the fighting scouts—grey, dour-looking craft that went flashing Up into the heavens at all hours of the day, some singly, some in orderly methodical squadrons. Theirs was usually a roving commission. They wandered whither they would and when they would, without order and without question.

This meagre 8 *per cent.*, who alone of many thousands of pilots were qualified to undertake the strenuous business of aerial combat, made as many years' history in as few days. Of them, one official etiquette demands his identity be no more revealed than a "certain pilot"—met two unwary Huns a-roaming; which brought his bag of Boche machines to twenty-one. A further victim swelled his list the following afternoon. And the ensuing twenty-four hours of rain only left him more eager and determined for the one great adventure of the "push."

At 10,500 feet—exactly two miles high, he skirted the clouds in the early sunshine, waiting and watching. Below, a squadron of six Hun bombers swept past in an orderly line.

Of those who serve the air is demanded instant determination. Machines and men must move with celerity that is bewildering to the landsman. The three miles an hour of the infantryman is the sixty, the eighty, the hundred of the airman. Planning his action as he dived, that certain pilot took the enemy formation above and slightly in rear. His first half-drum of bullets brought a leading machine tumbling and spinning out of the line. Another dropped out of the fight, to make her base with a bullet-ridden wing.

By this time the Britisher had shot ahead, with four machine guns trained full on his back. Nevertheless, he wheeled back into the fight again, accounting for a further victim. Which necessitated, by every rule of Hun warfare, the remainder switching their tails for home.

With an unimpeded airway, the reports the reconnaissance pilots and observers brought in varied as widely as the front they circled. The information grew more concrete, more definite, as day succeeded day. Like a "movie" picture, the scenes flashed on to the screen in proper sequence. First came the enemy labour battalions, swarming like ants below, busy about the concrete bases for the heavy guns, which arrived in due course—deadly and disgruntled, on trucks drawn by puffing tractors.

Infantry—from 10,000 feet, shapeless, sprawling masses of grey—choked every roadway leading up to the direction of the lines; accompanying them the customary columns of supply. Some twenty miles across the lines an observer jubilantly wirelessed home the discovery of a new 17-inch howitzer position. Five miles east and out of his sight another reconnaissance machine had detected the advance of considerable enemy reinforcements. From yet another quarter there came the welcome news of the discovery of a new enemy ammunition dump. And from another, "Nothing to report"—this the most significant news of any. That particular area would be kept under closer observation than any in the near future.

The movements of the enemy were watched and a great many hostile batteries were located and reported to our artillery.

Adventures attendant on these manoeuvres were many and varied. In his own peculiar phraseology, a wounded officer of the R.F.C.:

They saw something doing in the rear of the Hun lines, flew down to have a closer look, and came under the fire of some 'Archies.' A direct hit smashed the engine. The pilot didn't lose control, but planed down as much in the direction of the British line as he could. They came to earth inside the Boche lines, unhurt, nipped out of the ruined 'bus' pretty quick, and started running in the direction of the British trenches.

After running for some time, they spotted a sort of erection affair, like a big gun-pit. They crept closer and heard the Boches talking. It was a gun-pit. So, they squatted down and made a sketch map of it, with a bearing or two to get the proper range. After that they crept and ran and crawled until they got to the back of the canal. They had to swim for it, and as they left the bank a couple of Boche snipers got a bead on them, and they had just time to locate the beggars hiding in sunken barrels before they dived. They swum under water, coming up for a breather now and then, with the Boche snipers blazing away, but they got through all right. While still dressed only in wet shirts they got on the 'phone to our heavies, and gave the exact location of that gun-pit, as well as the two barrels. Next thing that happened was a series of direct hits on that gun emplacement and the two snipers' barrels were sent sky-high.

Bit by bit, item by item, these reports were all pieced together. To the staff officer, running through the observers' reports with his map, the country revealed itself, army corps by army corps, gun by gun, and trench by trench, until he knew exactly what areas required the attention of our artillery and what could be ignored. And if the staff was the head that directed affairs, no less were the aircraft the eye and the brain that supplied the directions. The two work always in the closest co-operation. A chance aerial report shows up at G.H.Q. Commotion is immediate. Along the wires is flashed the news up to Divisional Head-quarters. More commotion; more consultation. Then a telephone-bell tinkles somewhere miles ahead. The bombardment has begun.

In the marionette show of the great game of war the figures—the infantry in the frontline trenches and the heavies immediately behind them—only move to the manipulation of the wires by the staff at G.H.Q. There is the power centre that gives life, by way of innumer-able lines, to these smouldering masses.

In the matter of artillery bombardment aircraft were again indis-pensable. Before the batteries opened fire the aeroplane would be cir-cling over the objective; and when the bombardment opened, they commenced wirelessing back to the battery the positions of the bursts of their shells; thuswise, "Your last shot over," or "short of," or "too much to the left or right."

On the other hand, some positions were too far distant to be shelled. These it would be necessary to raid. Manoeuvres of this na-ture were mostly carried out during the night. And that was the most difficult flying work of all. X. Squadron realised this fact to its fullest extent.

Setting off in the darkness, with a highly explosive cargo aboard, the pilots would have to literally feel their way, with no landmark to guide them to their objectives.

At the low altitude at which they flew they were liable, at any moment, to be picked up by a German searchlight and shot down to earth. Having reached their objective and having dropped their bombs, they had yet to make the return journey and land in the dark.

Daylight raids were few and far between. But, such as they were, the Boche had an admirable object-lesson set him—that, in this most barbarous form of warfare of the ages, there were yet finer and more delicate distinctions. The British pilots, in order to bomb the true objectives and not to massacre helpless civilians, came unusually low, in grave risk of their own necks, and rarely missed their mark. From a height of little above the lines of telegraph-wires alongside the railway that "certain pilot" of X. Squadron cheerfully strafed a convoy, and a moment later lessened his machine of the weight of several drums of bullets, placing same into both sets of windows of a troop train, and inflicting many casualties.

The enemy's guns continued their delicate attentions all along the line, but were unable to prevent him from bombing another train in a siding. The engine of the latter rocked off the rails at the shock of the first impact, the driver giving obvious refutation to the theory that German dignity never takes to its heels. The quick eye of the pilot caught sight of numerous boxes in the trucks. Ammunition, he thought. From a height of fifteen feet, he sprayed them with shot; but without result. Again, he returned; still nothing happened.

Somewhat apologetic he afterwards explained the situation to the commanding officer. "Heavens, man!" exclaimed the latter, "did it never strike you what would have happened if you had hit that ammunition?"

"I'm afraid it didn't, sir." The pilot blushed; he was very young. In the ensuing "push" that certain train fell into the hands of the British. Therein high explosive was piled up from end to end.

By this time the push was almost ready to begin. The fighting scouts were turned out to scour the skies in all directions. Now, more than at any time, it was necessary to keep the enemy from the air. One German machine overhead would discover the movement, put his corps commander on his guard, and lead our men into ambush instead of victory.

The condition of the air was particularly unhealthy. Anti-aircraft shells, rifle bullets, artillery shells, small and great, were bursting all round. Were one of the latter—say, a 15-inch—to hit a machine, it would simply vanish into thin air.

Yet while all this was going on the aeroplane pilot had, perforce, to keep in touch with the infantry, watch how the push proceeded, and constantly report progress to headquarters, thus proving that aircraft were indispensable to any stage of the modern battle.

In the next day's newspapers appeared a glowing account of an advance of threequarters of a mile on an eight-mile front. The X. Squadron of the R.F.C. figured largely in a subsequent field-marshal's despatch. The commanding officer got his D.S.O. And for that "certain pilot" arrived one day, by motor orderly, a thin buff slip, on which was scrawled in faded pencil:

Well done!—D.H.

CHAPTER 12

Work and Development of the Royal Flying Corps

The remarkable feature of the R.F.C. apart from its development is that it is the outcome of the genius and foresight of a single man Lieutenant-General Sir David Henderson, K.C.B., D.S.O. As a Brigadier, Sir David took as early a flying certificate as No. 118, and when the R.F.C. was officially constituted in June 1912 he was immediately appointed Director of Military Aeronautics.

In those times the Flying Corps comprised both Naval and Military wings; and controlled aeroplanes, balloons, and airships alike. But the chief occupation of the Director appeared to be that of obtaining the necessary finance from conservative-minded politicians who regarded aviation as a wild sport for adventurous young men. What Sir David accomplished on that miserable pittance would open the eyes of a company-promoter wide with envy.

Thus, after the R.N.A.S., on July 1st, 1914, had been constituted a separate body, and when, a month prior to the war, a concentration of R.F.C. squadrons was held on Salisbury Plain, no more than five squadrons could be assembled. And they aggregated forty-odd machines!

By borrowing motor transport and machines from the Central Flying School this total was raised—so Lord Curzon informed us, in his tribute to the Flying Services, in the House of Lords, October 29th, 1917—to sixty-six machines and 100 flying officers.

Not one of these machines possessed a greater horse-power than eighty, speed of more than seventy miles an hour, or a British-built engine. Yet they all flew across to France without mishap—a great feat in those days. And forty-eight hours later they were in operation on the western front.

What has been accomplished in the interval may best be judged by a further reference to Lord Curzon's speech:

It all seemed like the survival of the romance of a bygone age. The 100 flying officers and few machines we possessed at the outbreak of war had grown into an enormous fleet consisting of thousands of machines and tens of thousands of men.

By the statement of Major Baird, in the House of Commons, that:

There are now 958 firms engaged with work for the Director of Aeronautical Supplies—301 as direct contractors, and 657 as sub-contractors, with a possible output of sixteen machines per month apiece.

Taking this to be the average output, the yearly aggregate would be 57,792 machines! And by the fact that most months—sometimes weeks—we lose more aeroplanes than constituted the original Expeditionary Force.

Vast as has been the development of the sister service, R.N.A.S., it can in no way compare to that of the R.F.C. The latter is now a great army in itself. The Commander is a major-general, who, as Director-General of Military Aeronautics, is *ex-officio* member of the Army Council, and:

Is responsible to the Secretary of State for so much of the business relating to the administration of the Army Air Service as is not subject to the control of either the Air Board or the Ministry of Munitions, and as may be assigned to him from time to time by the Secretary of State.

A day rarely goes by without some reference to the work of the airmen in the Headquarters Official. And the corps has been honoured by the king as colonel-in-chief; while aerodromes have sprung up in every county and district in the United Kingdom. At one time, at a large aerodrome may be seen as many machines in the air as constituted the original Flying Corps. And there are more aeroplanes flying over Great Britain today than there are motorcars running in the streets!

The Flying Corps has developed for the most part at home; where it now also combines the duties of home defence against raiding aircraft, and supplies craft and personnel to the armies on the western front, Salonica, Palestine, India, Italy, Mesopotamia, South and British East Africa. Aircraft factories have sprung up literally in hundreds, each employing thousands of skilled mechanics and trained women. Dozens of officers and hundreds of men are employed at every aerodrome. The Air Board itself necessitates a small army of experts, secretaries, orderlies, and clerks. The Aviation Inspection Department may be numbered in thousands. And the Air Services now claim a separate financial estimate.

The corps is sub-divided into wings, squadrons, and flights; each with its own Commander. The personnel is composed of pilots, observers, photographers, wireless experts, balloon pilots, equipment officers, engineers, trained mechanics, and women the last being supplied by the Women's Army Auxiliary Corps.

ADMINISTRATION

Sir David Henderson continued to be in command of the R.F.C. until October 12th, 1917, when it was announced by the Secretary of the War Office that:

> Having been deputed to undertake special work, he had been lent for such services, and had thereby vacated his seat on the Army Council.

The announcement continued that:

> The Secretary of State for War had appointed Major-General J. M. Salmond as his successor as Director-General of Military Aeronautics, with a seat on the Army Council.

At the same time Major-General Brancker, Deputy Director of Military Aeronautics, was appointed to a command abroad, and for the present, it was further announced, his place would not be filled, thus leaving the original Headquarters Staff with:

> *Director.*—Brevet Lieutenant-Colonel L. C. O. Charlton, C.M.G., D.S.O., Lancashire Fusiliers.
> *Deputy Assistant Director.*—Major and Brevet Lieutenant-Colonel W. D. Dooner, Army Ordnance Dept.
> *Deputy Assistant Adjutant-General.*—Lieutenant (temporary Major) H. S. Ebben, R.F.C., S.R.
> *Staff Captain.*—Captain C. F. Gordon, M.C., North Lancashire Regiment.

Major-General Trenchard, who, from the time of Sir David Henderson's return to England in 1915, succeeded him as C.O. in the field, is still controlling the work of the R.F.C. in the war area, and is ably assisted by Temporary Brigadier-General E. L. Ellington, while Major-General Ashmore is responsible for the aerial defences of London.

On November 2nd it was announced by *The London Gazette* that the king has been pleased, by Letters Patent under the Great Seal of the United Kingdom of Great Britain and Ireland, bearing date October 18th, to appoint:

Major and Brevet Lieutenant-Colonel (temporary Major-General) John Maitland Salmond the new Director-General of Military Aeronautics, taking the place of Lieutenant-General Sir David Henderson, K.C.B., D.S.O.

In the Field

Leaving the matter of administration, let us turn again to the more practical side, that of the work of the R.F.C. in the field. We had left those 100 gallant pilots and their sixty-odd decrepit craft at the time of the first landing. Of their glorious achievement in holding the air, through many strenuous months, against the 600 well-equipped aeroplanes with which the enemy took the field; of the reconnaissance pilot who first brought news to Sir H. Smith-Dorrien that his advanced division was faced by three German Army Corps; of the British aircraft whose timely information saved the Allies, and the world, in that historic retreat from Mons, and of many other inimitable deeds of the pilots of the R.F.C., we have heard and read on countless occasions.

(*Vide Smith-Dorrien* by Horace Smith-Dorrien, the long career of a great soldier: Leonaur 2009.)

There is no need for us to dwell upon that glorious chapter of British history; that opened the book at the Aisne, and turned the last page at that bloody second Battle of Ypres. The years of nineteen fourteen, fifteen, and sixteen marked a period of remarkable evolution in aviation. Some sort of policy had, perforce, to be formulated that dealt comprehensively with this latest form of warfare. The nucleus of a great personnel had to be established and developed to maintain the ever-growing expansion. Types of new machines had to be experimented, constructed, tested; and adopted or discarded. And reconnaissance, direction of artillery, wireless telegraphy, aerial gunnery, photography, and bomb-dropping had to be placed upon some suitable basis.

I repeat: the first three years of the war were merely a period of evolution as regards aviation. It was not until the spring of 1917 that aerial warfare naturally developed. And proof of this assertion may be amplified by a reference to Sir Douglas Haig's daily reports from Headquarters, and from the fact that 717 aeroplanes—of all nations— were destroyed in April and 713 in June alone.

The progress achieved by the R.F.C. in this matter may best be judged—from an unintentional tribute—a report written by a commander in the 31st German Infantry Regiment, which was captured by our troops north of the Ancre. Describing the bombardment of his trench, he says:

> Enemy airmen were over our position the whole day and came down very low. They directed the fire throughout. Our own artillery seems to have fired very little. German airmen appeared only towards evening, but the enemy's airmen would not let themselves be disturbed in their work. Nothing is left of the trench.

In every big battle of the year aircraft have played a prominent part. Thus, we find an expert French commentator, on March 22nd, 1917, after the advance, writing:

> Despite bad weather, there was considerable air activity in the zone of the enemy's retreat. French and British aviators furnished their general staffs with most valuable information, and successfully drove off many enemy machines.

Again, concerning the big push round Bapaume, Mr. Philip Gibbs gives the following glimpses of the work of the R.F.C.:

> Flights of British aeroplanes were up and singing with a loud deep humming music, as of monstrous bees. Our Archies were strafing a German 'plane, venturesome over our country. High up in the blue was the rattle of machine-gun fire. . . .
> The Germans have a cavalry screen behind their rearguards. They were seen yesterday north of Bapaume and southwards beyond Roye. And some of them were chased by a British airman at a place called Ennemain. He swooped low like an albatross, and brought a man off his horse by a machine-gun bullet. Others stampeded from this terrible bird.

In the advance, towards the end of April, Sir Douglas Haig made constant references to the activity of the airmen. And Mr. Beach Thomas, in *The Daily Mail*, sums the whole affair up as follows:

We have never before hit the German so hard or so harassed him by day and night. A night or two ago our men broke up three trains near Douai, one after the other, with bombs dropped from a couple of hundred feet, and so terrified soldiers and other officials with the rattle of machine-guns that the attackers escaped with scarcely an attempt at resistance. A day later two of our fighting 'planes which had sought the Germans in vain for several previous days suddenly came upon a fleet of fourteen ... charged this motley group, broke up the formation, and sent two crashing to the ground.

The enemy's losses in purely fighting machines are enormously greater than ours. His plan when he attacks is to mass his 'planes against a single observer, knowing that most observing 'planes are no match for the fighter. . . .

We hold again the mastery of the air. Whether we keep it depends, first and foremost, on the activity of the factories at home. As I was listening at the aerodrome to a stirring tale of a duel that lasted for half an hour, a speck was seen in the air and the first home-comer of a patrol of three was recognised. He landed and 'taxied' up to us. The clouds had been too low for good flying. He had had no adventures, he said, and was home first because the engine was giving a little trouble. Then he looked over the machine and saw what we had already seen—a huge rent and a broken wire in the body of the 'plane. Clearly a great lump of shrapnel had struck a yard or two behind his back. We had the explanation presently when another two returned. The neighbour pilot had seen an extra double-sized shrapnel shell from an anti-aircraft gun burst just between the two of them—an alarming fact, of which the younger pilot had been wholly unaware.

Evidence accumulates of the depression caused among the enemy's infantry by the activity of our airmen. A German document describes the moral effect on infantry of balloons 'hanging like grapes in clusters' and watching every movement below.

A yet more complete survey of a period of R.F.C. work on the western front was furnished by the Military Correspondent of *The Times*, in the first of his series of special articles:

In four months before Arras our aeroplanes reported 1,589 direct hits on German guns, as well as some 200 important explosions, so that the German administration, which was already hard put to it to repair its guns, to create a reserve, and to provide artillery for the new divisions, must have had an anxious time. . . .

I only saw two German aeroplanes cross our lines during my visit to the British front, and when some of ours came up and drove them off I thought that ours looked like thoroughbreds and the German hackneys. There were, however, plenty of German aeroplanes on the German side of the line, as well as many observation balloons. The Fokker is fairly played out on the western front, where the Albatross one-seater and the Halberstadter represent the best single-seater fighting machines of the enemy. The former has two guns firing through the propeller and a 160 h.p. Mercedes engine. The Roland, the L.V.G., the Rumpler, and the Aviatik are the most common two-seater 'planes.

Fighting, reconnaissance, and artillery work are carried out by separate units, and a sharp distinction is drawn between these different spheres of aerial activity. The organisation of the German Air Service is fairly well known to us, and we also know to our cost that we were met by superior numbers of fast single-seater fighting machines at the opening of this year's campaign.

On June 8th, after the taking of the Messines Ridge, Field-Marshal Sir Douglas Haig congratulated the R.F.C. in the following terms:

Following on the great care and thoroughness in the preparations made under the orders of General Sir Herbert Plumer, the complete success gained may be ascribed chiefly to the destruction caused by our mines, to the violence and accuracy of our bombardment, to the very fine work of the R.F.C., and to the incomparable dash and courage of the infantry.

While, towards the end of the summer—August 28th—*The Daily Mail* published a dispatch from Mr. Beach Thomas, describing what must have been a record week in the air. Said Mr. Thomas:

I have just read the summing-up of a week's journeyman's work by our Flying Corps in France, and it so excels all that is on record in fact, or indeed in fiction, that I will omit the stirring tales of all individual adventures in favour of a mere naked epitome. The properest work of the airmen in war is the finding of the enemy's guns and directing fire on them. That is what matters most, though it is the least dramatic in telling, and it is chiefly in this department that past experience has been excelled.

From August 14th to 21st our airmen helped the guns to range on well over 700 German batteries. They and the gunners worked so well together that 128 gun-pits were totally destroyed, and among the batteries 321 separate explosions were caused.

The figures indicate the immense scale of the artillery fighting, as well as of aerial observation. Indeed, such now is the intensity of the gunfire that what is called a counter-attack does not necessarily imply any movement of infantry at all.

Under good observation from the enemy it may be as dangerous for the field gunners to fire as for infantry to go over the parapet. At the same time unobserved gunners can drive back the infantry without the need of help from their own infantry. Such experiences have been common in the last few weeks. In the recent fighting the gunners have had almost the same sensation of a hand-to-hand battle as the charging infantry, and have needed the same sort of courage and calmness.

In places the Germans, though they have lost their so-called grand stands or super-observation points, as Vimy and Hill 70 and Messines and Pilkem Ridge, have still one or two ridges which force all the duty of observation on our airmen.

As to the rest of this unparalleled week in our airmen's records let the bare figures speak for themselves. They flew in the week over 1,200 hours; they took another 5,000 photographs of the enemy's territory; they dropped over 2,000 bombs, amounting to about thirty-six tons in weight; they fired more than 30,000 rounds from low levels at the enemy's infantry and gunners; they brought down sixty-eight enemy 'planes, and are known for a certainty to have driven down ninety more, of which a great number were certainly destroyed.

It must be remembered that our authorities are as strict as an adverse judge in sifting the evidence of crashed machines. Many not recorded even as hit are crashed, as later evidence has often proved. The German airmen, rather like the German gunners, have been braver at night than by day. They have bombed many places, from hospitals to harvest fields.

The most important reference to the R.F.C, of the year, however, was contained in a long dispatch from Sir Douglas Haig, concerning the battle of the Somme.

Writing of the German trenches between the Somme and the Ancre, Sir Douglas Haig says:

The second system itself, in many places, could not be observed from the ground in our possession, while, except from the air, nothing could be seen of his more distant defences. . . .

On June 25th the R.F.C. carried out a general attack on the enemy's observation balloons, destroying nine of them, and depriving the enemy for the time being of this form of observation. . . .

On the same day (September 26th) Gueudecourt was carried, after the protecting trench to the west had been captured in a somewhat interesting fashion. In the early morning a tank started down the portion of the trench held by the enemy from the north-west, firing its machine-guns and followed by bombers. The enemy could not escape, as we held the trench at the southern end. At the same time an aeroplane flew down the length of the trench, also firing a machine-gun at the enemy holding it. These then waved white handkerchiefs in token of surrender, and when this was reported by the aeroplane the infantry accepted the surrender of this garrison. By 8.30 a.m. the whole trench had been cleared, great numbers of the enemy had been killed, and eight officers and 362 other ranks made prisoners. Our total casualties amounted to five.

In this combination between infantry and artillery the R.F.C. played a highly important part. The admirable work of this Corps has been a very satisfactory feature of the battle. Under the conditions of modern war, the duties of the Air Service are many and varied. They include the regulation and control of artillery fire by indicating targets and observing and reporting the results of rounds; the taking of photographs of enemy trenches, strong points, battery positions, and of the effect of bombardments; and the observation of the movements of the enemy behind his lines.

The greatest skill and daring has been shown in the performance of all these duties, as well as in bombing expeditions. Our Air Service has also co-operated with our infantry in their assaults, signalling the position of our attacking troops, and turning machineguns on to the enemy infantry and even on to his batteries in action.

Not only has the work of the R.F.C. to be carried out in all weathers and under constant fire from the ground, but fighting in the air has now become a normal procedure, in order to maintain the mastery over the enemy's Air Service. In these fights the greatest skill and determination have been shown, and great success has attended the efforts of the R.F.C. I desire to point out, however, that the maintenance of mastery of the air, which is essential, entails a constant and liberal supply of the most up-to-date machines, without which even the most skilful pilots cannot succeed.

A happy augury for the future of the lately formed R.A.F.

CHAPTER 13

Moonlight Over the Battle

If you really want to know what our flying men are doing over there, avoid reading the Daily Officials. They recount little enough to satisfy even a British Board of Censors. Should sense of duty compel you so to do, it is between the lines that history is steeped. It is the commas that are often likely clues, and the full-stops that reveal whole chapters. Here are two of them with, packed between, in terse phrasing, the makings of a sensational "romantic novel."

Two of our aeroplanes which were reported missing in the *communiqués* of the last two days have since returned to their squadrons.

Never a word as to what occurred in that trying ordeal of the twenty-four-hour interval. Again:

Sixteen of our machines have not yet been located. Many of these have undoubtedly made forced landings behind our lines owing to the difficulty of finding their aerodromes in the heavy rain.—(like the wordless film version of a great sensational play.)

Who wishes to get to grips with that adventurous spirit that animates the air must himself essay the terrors and the joys of the airmen. One must go racing up to the sky when the first flush of dawn is in the east, the icy blast worming into one's bones; the earth surface opening out on all sides like the petals of a new-blown rose; when the sudden storm comes squalling up from interminable space; when the light is blotted out by the darkness of night. That is the time when the vast shadows harbour friend and foe in every yard, danger and adventure in every mile. Follow that squadron there sweeping across the British trenches, their powerful engines echoing and re-echoing along the still grey lines for miles on either hand, a night bombing expedition on its outward way.

The night is black—black as a raven's wing. The moon has not yet come up; the stars are cloaked behind an impenetrable canopy. But the faintest pin-heads of light indicate the raiders' locality. As they come up, with a gradually increasing audibleness, they fill the skies with a tumultuous roaring and then die away into the dark uncertainty of No-Man's Land ahead.

Their squadron commander is at their head. In rear of him—keeping precise and well-ordered formation—ride six cumbersome "bombers," loaded heavily with high explosives. Another fighting scout hovers on the extreme left; now darting out in the darkness toward some suspicious light; now diving in to regain formation. Some faint quivering signal flashes in from the leader. They are well over the enemy's country by now, and must climb to avoid possible antiaircraft traps. Eight blunt noses veer upwards simultaneously. The combined roar of eight engines dies away perceptibly.

Almost too late; red, angry bursts pepper the blackness; murderous, whining shrieks make themselves audible, even above the racing motors. The squadron hesitates, loses formation, regains it, and flies on. The battle-plane on the left dives down, headlong, at the flashing gun-mouths. A bomb or so goes hurtling down into the night, awakening the quietened countryside with murderous detonations. And then, when all danger seems to be passed, the leader suddenly lunges down out of position; rolling and quivering, like a wounded bird.

A hostile searchlight focuses him, bringing him well within sight of his pack, until, 1,000 feet lower, he regains control; turns with a sharp bank, and heads towards his base. His squadron flies on, leaving in rear a renewed burst of firing, and a sky slashed and lined with innumerable searchlights. Instinct whispers them to wheel to his aid; duty, to carry on ahead. Their orders are definite.

Left to his own devices, the leader clears the bombardment, slithers out of searchlight range, and brings his battered 'plane to earth between the opposing lines of trenches. Travelling at well over sixty miles an hour across the hillocky surface, his machine suddenly tilts nose-foremost into a deep shell-hole. There is a crash of splintering wings and woodwork; the force of the collision starts off a bomb.

Soon—very soon—the declivity is a mass of burning wreckage. Fighting for life, the pilot manages to extricate himself, and scramble up on to the surface. His leather flying-coat well alight, his eyes and throat choked with smarting, blinding smoke, he rolls over and over on the ground to the banks of a tiny stream, tumbles in, and loses consciousness, as several dark figures come swarming over the top of the British trenches. There is a rapid exchange of rifle shots with the enemy infantry, who have also witnessed the catastrophe, and they hurriedly pick him up and carry him back to their own trenches.

That sunset hour is the busiest of the airman's whole twenty-four. Before the light goes west occurs that tense ceremony of watching the birds come "winging home to roost." From time to time, during the day, pilots have been reported missing. Sundown is the last call. If the missing man doesn't come slithering in at sundown, the chances are that he will never return at all.

Anxious groups—making believe with laughter and fooling—gather on the aerodrome; counting the tiny black shapes, one by one, as they show up on the sky-line; tally them in their minds until the last man has landed safely; and then move off towards the Mess. Never before!

After sunset, when the turmoil of the day-battle, the roaring hubbub of the guns, and the distant crackle of rifle fire, have died away, when the first trench rockets hiss skywards, in a spluttering trail of light, these aerodromes, free of the resonant hum of mighty engines and bustle of mechanics and pilots, are strangely forlorn in appearance.

But farther back are other similar aerodromes, not so deserted. Their wide spaces are filled with throbbing engines. The ground is ablaze with the flares of labouring mechanic squads. All day there has been a stillness on their spacious enclosures. Only at the time of sunset do they liven up. For these are the aerodromes of the night-raiding aeroplanes, which steal away in the darkness to bomb enemy dumps and communications.

Great powerful machines stretch wing to wing across the enclosure; their parts specially constructed to neutralise the reflective power of metals; gleaming dully in the light of the flares. Opposite the pilot's seat in each 'plane, the instrument-board is illuminated by carefully screened electric glow-lamps, and hardly a glimmer comes above the cockpit even when all the higher lights are shining, and though the pilot can distinguish every pointing indicator as it moves across the dials as clearly as by the light of day.

The pilots appear from their quarters, and stroll towards their machines. They are heavily clad—much more heavily than their fellows of the daylight. The night is cold, and they have farther to go; so, they take precautions. The chorus of the final engine tuning-up greets them as they approach, and mechanics scramble out from beneath wings and fuselages, leaving the bomb-racks well filled and in order.

The pilots clamber into their places. The engine hum becomes a roar, one by one the machines start forward over the enclosure and glide upwards into the night. Red and white identification lights on each wing-tip show for a little, a galaxy of new stars; and then this last sigh of their presence also disappears as the squadron heads swiftly for the distant line.

Their course is as direct as a ruled line: over the trenches, with all their wavering display of starshells, and on into the enemy's country, where all manner of adventures waylay their speeding feet. Long beams of enemy searchlights stab the darkness, seeking them among the upper shadows. Occasionally finding a 'plane and dazzling her pilot with their brilliant concentration. Occasionally holding such feats of arms as:

Two British machines, convoying a raiding-party, north of, and over St. J——, encountered seven Hun fighting-scouts. Pilot number one put down three of them with just over two drums of ammunition; his companion immediately being attacked by the other four. He brought down one, and then, after pretending to escape, suddenly executed a sharp "volte face" and attacked a second machine, which was forced down. At that moment a machine-gun bullet glanced off the British captain's motor, and he was forced to descend out of the fight. A big German machine tried to bar his way, but the discharge of 150 machine-gun bullets quickly forced the monster to make a compulsory descent to earth; and both British craft flew back to rejoin their squadron.

But, however glaring the searchlight may be, the British pilot soon recovers. He pulls back his control lever, and climbing upwards, leaves the Archie clusters bursting beneath him. Then, strange snakelike flashes quiver and disappear over the horizon of the sky.

These flashes—unwisely enough—indicate the positions of the enemy aerodromes. They are caused by the Huns firing a fixed number of green balls, string-fashion, into the sky, which—in addition to their aerial lighthouses—assist the raiders when returning to their bases. From a height of 10,000 feet those fired from the Belgian coast can actually be seen by German machines high over London, who then have only to steer in the direction of these recurrent signals to "hit" their coast at a known spot.

Leaving searchlights, green balls, and antiaircraft shells behind them, the British squadron at last sights the faint glow of a darkened

German city far below, which tells the pilots that the objective has been reached.

Circling round to pick up their targets the big 'planes look like gaunt night vampires searching for their prey. A sudden jerk of a pilot's hand and half a ton of bombs go hurtling earthward. A large flash, a dull boom, and then a steady glow. And far away from the confusion and panic reigning below in that stricken German town, the great machines swing round in the vastness of the heavens, and, amid a halo of bursting shell, head for the line and home—the record of the affair being set forth in the next day's British Official somewhat after the following manner:

> Following on the successful daylight raids on the 18th inst., against Treves and Thionville, our night-flying squadrons went out after dark and again attacked these towns from a low height with equally good results. Five bursts were observed on Treves station, which broke into flames. Three other buildings were alight when our machines left. In the second raid on Thionville, bursts were seen on the railway and in the gasworks. A large fire was started which was visible to the pilots attacking Treves. German aircraft and anti-aircraft guns were very active during both raids. One of our machines failed to return.

Meanwhile, as these happenings are toward, the enemy is also out scouring the skies. Probably he is bombing London. The stories of the thrilling fights which then occur with British aircraft would fill a volume. Here is one typical instance that occurred late in the autumn of last year.

A Gotha was trapped by a British machine over the centre of the city. Another Britisher tacked into the fight, a moment later. The searchlights caught and held them. In and out, darting all over the place, twisting and turning with bewildering speed, the British aeroplanes looked like bringing down the Hun any moment. It was the sight of a lifetime for old London—common enough maybe on the front, but a unique thrill over the house-tops. More than once it seemed that the Hun was surely vanquished. It seemed so as the others shot out like a flash, changed their tactics in a twinkling, wriggled, squirmed, and tested their opponent in every conceivable manner.

To see the race for higher levels—a race to be top dog, in a double sense—was the sort of thing that made you hold your breath. To watch the British machines cut in and hurl their machine-gun charges at the singlehanded fighter made you want to cheer.

The German was a fighter—give him his due. He responded in kind, so far as firing went. He made a desperate struggle for life; the issue was in doubt, with the odds decidedly against the enemy, up to the last moment. Then, with a start, one of the British machines was in at close quarters. A little flicker of red flame burst out at the nose of the Hun machine. The next moment he was plunging headlong for earth. But he fell wide, clear of the city.

And of another raiding Gotha which was brought down in flames in the Isle of Thanet, it is recounted by an infantry officer, who went out to look for the crew, that the pilot was discovered a quarter of an hour later, wandering aimlessly across a field. He made no attempt at resistance. He was too frozen cold to think of such a thing. His face was a greyish blue; his fingers numbed and lifeless; almost unable to walk, he stumbled across to the British officer, and pulled up short.

Between his numbed lips was an unlighted cigarette. He said never a word; merely indicating his "smoke" with a movement of his hand; followed by a pantomimic exhibition of striking a match.

The Britisher hesitated; looked hard at him for a second or so, then, fumbling in his pockets, produced the desired match and lit his cigarette.

CHAPTER 14

Aces And Pawns

"Ace" is a war word and, moreover, one peculiar to flying circles. "Champion," "star," "crack," call him what you will, an "ace" is a pilot who has accounted to his "bag" five or more enemy craft. He is your knight-errant, genius, athletic god in one. But unlike other athletic gods, his prowess is not constituted solely of beef and brawn. He may be—and in fact often has been—delicate of physique, and lacking in physical powers. Guynemer was a noteworthy example. And he was the "ace of aces."

Of the latter the belligerent Flying Services have, so far, produced not more than seven. On the British side there have been Ball, Bishop, and McCudden. Boelke and von Richthofen, the elder, were the German stars. And France rejoiced in the inimitable Guynemer, with Nungesser a worthy successor. James Byford McCudden's was the most romantic career of any. He had won every possible British decoration—the V.C., the D.S.O. (twice), the M.C., the M.M., and possesses in addition the French *Croix de Guerre*.

A modest youth, with an attractive personality, he typified the clean-built, sporting Englishman, descended from a fighting stock. For his father—a typical Irishman—was a warrant officer in the Royal Engineers, and his father's father and grandfather were soldiers before him. His mother also was a "soldier" woman, with martial father and grandfather before her. One brother—the eldest of a trio—had already given his life in the service of the air. Another bids fair to, someday, improve upon John Byford's record. And yet another, of sixteen years of age, has already joined up with the R.F.C.

McCudden, who until recently was leader of a squadron which has accounted for ninety-nine Boche machines, was only twenty-three. He joined the British Army as a private in a regiment of the line, eight years ago; transferring to the Flying Corps in 1912, to the old balloon section. In the stress of the German rush through Belgium,

Air-Mechanic McCudden, having had some experience in the air, was pressed into service at Mons as an observer. For excellent services there displayed, he was granted a commission. And from that to his captaincy was no long step.

While yet in the ranks he won renown for his handling of the guns in several stiff fights, and was awarded the *Croix de Guerre* and the Military Medal. The official account of the great deed was:

> For consistent gallantry, courage, and dash during the month of September 1916, in attacking and destroying an enemy machine, and forcing two others to land.
> He also twice crossed the enemy lines at a very low altitude in attacks on hostile balloons under very heavy fire.

And on another occasion, he dived down after a hostile machine to a height of only 300 feet and drove it to the ground.

Over a hundred fights he waged against Boche airmen. Three times he fought the redoubtable Immelmann to a standstill; and on every occasion the fight had to be broken off owing to both men running out of ammunition. He paid Immelmann the tribute of being "a great airman, and a gallant fighter."

Another R.F.C. pilot once remarked of him:

> McCudden is one of the real geniuses of aerial fighting. He has established enough theories to fill a volume.

McCudden himself told me that his invariable method was to dive for the enemy's tail. And in this way, he estimated that he had accounted for no less than forty-seven of his "bag." He was more than enthusiastic about the future. But as he so characteristically remarked:

> We must get on with the war, before we can find time to think about anything else.

Comparing his total with the "aces" of either nations, we find that his name figures second on the list. Here is the order of them: von Richthofen (German), 74; McCudden (Britain), 57; Guynemer (France), 53; Bishop (Britain), 47; Fallard (Britain), 42; Nungesser (France), 31; and Fonck (France), 30. Nungesser is the French "*doyen de la chasse.*" He is a veteran at the game, and was France's leading battle pilot until Guynemer appeared upon the scene.

The French have the most rigorous method of calculating successes. A Boche machine is only "brought down" when it is seen to crash to earth on this side of the French lines. There is the keenest rivalry between the French pilots for first place; and there are several youngsters who are running Nungesser close. The latter, by the way, every time he crosses the lines seeks out some vanquisher of a former comrade who has fallen in the field of battle.

Last December the engine of Nungesser's machine failed when at a great height, and the machine crashed to the ground. By a miracle he escaped himself, but his mechanic was killed outright. Badly shaken as he was, yet he refused to take any leave in order not to lose his proud position of "ace of the aces."

Fonck held him neck and neck, with thirty apiece, until the end of January, when the elder man encountered a German Albatross in the neighbourhood of Berry-au-Bac, and brought it down after a stiff fight. Unfortunately, the third witness necessary was not forthcoming, so Nungesser was not credited. But on March 10th he assured his position by bringing down a fresh victim, near Craonne.

Cavalry Captain von Richthofen was the elder of two brothers; both of them crack battle pilots, and both with a goodly total of Allied airmen to their credit. The captain had been at it for over fifteen months; having encountered at various times Guynemer, Ball, and Hawker—an early British crack—whom he sent down to his death. In his book, published in 1917, von Richthofen gives a graphic account of his many fights—though, unfortunately, they are all written in that bombastic, swaggering style peculiar to the Boche. He does not mention the fact in his book, but the German "ace" reports his own victories, in which he includes captive-balloons. And he hunts always with a squadron.

So, we have the "top-lines" in their order, and in their ways. But it must not necessarily be concluded that they make best part of the air-war history; many a startling adventure and hair-breadth escape occur to pilots outside that exclusive coterie. Airmen of whom the world-at-large has never heard—nor is ever likely to hear—are carrying this most novel form of warfare into the most outlandish districts, quietly and unsung. And in these most out-of-the-way spots the most out-of-the-way events befall. Here is one of them:

Lieutenant G——, with the British Air Forces in East Africa, gives in a letter to *Flight* a piquant narrative of the perils of an aviator flying over those vast tropic wastes. He writes:

Once when he went out to bomb a German ambush on the

Rufiji River, and engine trouble landed him in a bog with a broken propeller, it took him four days to make his way to a place of safety through the bush infested with wild animals. In the dusk he was confronted with an ugly black animal about four feet high, with vicious tusks. He climbed a tree and prepared to put in the night there. Later he opened his eyes and saw something like two green electric bulbs about thirty feet from the tree. They moved round it in a circle. This continued for forty-five minutes.

The tension was unbearable. I wanted to scream, shout, and yell all in one, but instead I burst out with 'The Admiral's Broom,' and with a full-throated bass I roared out the three verses. No applause, but a reward—the leopard slunk away. Why had I not thought of it before?

I went through my repertoire. I laughed as I finished 'Two Eyes of Grey.' It seemed so ridiculous. Then I got on to hymns, remembered four verses of 'O God, our help in ages past,' and sang the 'Amen' too. The whole thing had its ludicrous side.

Next morning whilst swimming a river he passed seven yards from a crocodile's mouth, but just reached the bank in time. Without food or arms—his only weapon of defence his nail scissors—his progress through the awful bush was about 100 yards an hour. His clothing was in ribbons, and his flesh exposed to the thorns, sword grass, and flies.

He swam seven more rivers that day and sank down exhausted under a green tree. He could hear a lion roaring about 500 yards way, and somewhat nearer the grunting of a hippopotamus.

Being exhausted I more or less lost consciousness for perhaps half an hour or so. Nothing short of a hippo charging could have made me climb a tree. Am afraid life had little to offer about that time.

Whilst lying here Lieutenant Garrood:

. . . .had the annoying experience of surveying two large baboons, the size of a small man, quarrelling over his trousers, now in threads, and among the tops of forty-foot trees.

It was not until he had passed another horrible day and equally terrible night in the bush that he at last was picked up by some natives, he adds:

Their eyes seldom left me. Undoubtedly, I was a strange sight—my legs bare and bleeding, my short vest sodden, dirty, and torn, no trousers of course, just a dirty sun helmet, a short stick in my right hand, and with four days' growth of beard on my dirty face.

Another youthful veteran, attacked by a fighting formation of Boches, fired into one machine, which turned over on its back and spun down out of control. Then he turned his attention to another, and fired 200 rounds into it. Suddenly it went into a spin and crashed. Out with a battle flight of our own the following day, he spun lower and fired, and added a further Hun to his bag. Then, to make full measure that day, he fired an observation balloon; and in the afternoon, finished the aggregate at four enemy aeroplanes and a balloon in three days.

On another occasion two British machines, photography bound, ran up against half a dozen of the enemy's. Strictly speaking, theirs was a non-combatant craft, but, annoyed at the interruption, they laid about the enemy with their machine-gun to such effect that in a very short time they had knocked out two of their attackers. The remainder then flew away; and they returned to their picture-making, in peace.

Recently our bombers achieved a direct hit on a German Army kinema with results which, according to a prisoner's story, were, as one would expect, disastrous. Immediately, the unspeakable Boche retaliated by bombing our hospitals and stretcher-bearers behind the lines.

But vengeance was swift and immediate, winged on the planes of a British battle-plane. The pilot shot down the largest machine of the party, and turned, at bay, to meet the remainder. Like an avalanche, they hurled themselves at his head. He appeared to be totally inactive. Nearer and nearer, they drove—until, when they were almost on top of him, he made a neat, clean loop over them; to the tune of two further casualties.

Sometimes these "stunts" find their way into *The London Gazette*; the narrative form is hardly what one would style heart-stirring. But judge for yourself; this:

While flying over the enemy's lines he was attacked by twelve hostile scouts and engaged four of them, one of which he destroyed. He was then attacked by another of the enemy machines, and, though his observer had been wounded, he succeeded in destroying it. His machine was then rendered almost uncontrollable by a shell, the right wing being almost shot off, but he succeeded in landing it in our front-line wire. He has destroyed five hostile machines and shown splendid courage and determination.

Or this:

He took part in many successful operations over the enemy's lines, in over twenty of which he acted as leader. On one occasion, when leading a bombing raid, his formation was heavily attacked by enemy aeroplanes. He shot one of them down, and brought back the whole of his formation safely. He also led a successful raid on an enemy aerodrome, and on several occasions obtained valuable photographs. He has accounted for two enemy aeroplanes with his front gun, and always showed great coolness, ability, and resource.

It is when the boys write themselves that one gets nearer to the spirit of the thing. Compare, for instance, the two latter statements with this extract from the letter from an unofficial "ace," somewhere in France:

I saw a fine thing between Templeaux and Peronne. The Germans were smashing on. Our squadron was returning to our base 'empty.' There was very hot stuff being pumped at us. We could see miles of Huns, our shells bursting everywhere among them.
Suddenly one of our scouts was winged. He dropped like a crippled pigeon at a tremendous pace, and crashed horribly. At once another chap swooped, landed, picked him up, swung his blades, jumped in, took 'her' off, and put his tail up to our lines. It was all the work of a minute, and one of the pluckiest things I've seen this week.
The chap was dead.

Again; another extract from another letter:

On Tuesday morning I saw a pretty bit of work.
Fully 25,000 Germans were advancing below—under our very eyes, 10,000 feet above—when from the direction of Chauny there swung round seven French fighting squadrons—105 machines—glinting in the sun.
They manoeuvred beautifully. Fancy, Jim! a hundred 'planes in

a vertical turn at once! They sprang a lovely E-flat note, and 50,000 German ears heard it.

It was laughable and tragic.

Down swooped the Frenchmen with a whiz. They spread fan-wise. A mighty crescent of 100-lb. bombs fell, then another, then small stuff. Hundreds upon hundreds were killed.

I saw 5,000 men flat on their faces at once hoping to escape. It was just awful.

There is heroism unexampled in those few lines, and—a greater thing—a soldier's praise, as only a soldier can give it, in an unadorned recital of plain fact. There is the quick roving eye of the airman that covers the half of a battlefield in a twinkling of time, and misses not the smallest detail; there is the lusty j oy of youth in his nerve-racking occupation; and there is the joy of the enthusiast in the execution of it.

This joy and the whole-hearted defiance of danger once prompted a youthful British airman, who landed one day in the arid wastes of Sinai through a hail of shrapnel, beside a hard-pressed, dust-grimed infantry column, to carry off a mortally wounded man to the nearest hospital—forty-four miles away across the desert—and by his prompt action saved a life; and also, it was responsible for the doughty deeds of four merry men recently recounted by A. A. M. in *Punch*. He says that:

'A' found an aerodrome and sprayed the machines with bullets. 'B' got under a German machine at 300 feet, and fired into his engine. 'B' peppered him down to 100 feet, where 'B's' gun jammed. 'A,' having finished with his aerodrome, took over the German and saw him down safely to the ground, where he crashed, both wings folding up."

'C' says he saw him "cartwheeled on his back." 'A' then sprayed bullets along a train, while 'B' sprayed Boches who were playing football. 'B' also attended to a single-horse transport and three groups of Boches. 'C' came back low along the roads shooting at ground targets. And 'A. -A.' gunfire was "severe on homeward flight."

But all these deeds fade into insignificance when compared with the one that gained for Squadron Commander Moon a championship of the Distinguished Service Order. The story of it is:

On January 6th, 1917, whilst on a reconnaissance flight over the Rufiji Delta with Commander the Hon. R. O. B. Bridgeman,

D.S.O., R.N., as observer, he was obliged by engine trouble to descend in one of the creeks, where it became necessary to destroy the seaplane to avoid the possibility of its being captured. For three whole days the two officers wandered about the delta in their efforts to avoid capture and to rejoin their ship. During this time, they had little or nothing to eat, and were continually obliged to swim across the creeks, the bush on the banks being impenetrable.

On the morning of January 7th, they constructed a raft of three spars and some latticed window frames. After paddling and drifting on this for the whole of January 7th and 8th, they were finally carried out to sea on the morning of the 9th, when Commander Bridgeman, who was not a strong swimmer, died of exhaustion and exposure. In the late afternoon Flight Commander Moon managed to reach the shore, and was taken prisoner by the Germans; but was eventually released from captivity on November 21st, 1917.

CHAPTER 15

Marvels of the Air

More wonderful adventures bechance in the air than were ever thought of on land or at sea. They happen at all altitudes—among the clouds, a few hundred feet above the ground, over the sea, and over the roof-tops; and at all hours of the day and night. One second Death lays the air pilot by the heels, the next he is flying clear in the heavens. For instance, imagine the sensations experienced by a British pilot engaging an enemy machine for over twenty minutes, to find that only her inherent stability carried her on—her pilot was dead, shot through the heart.

What everyday event can compare with that of another flyer, who was shot through the arm by an "Archie" fragment at 8,000 feet. He lost consciousness. When he came to again it was to find himself lying in a hospital bed. The machine had flown herself across the British lines, and landed in a meadow. Aeroplanes have been employed frequently as Red Cross ambulances. Badly wounded men have been carried from behind the lines to the base hospitals in record time. An airman who was badly injured in a false landing outside a town on the north-east coast was attended by a doctor who arrived in another 'plane. And, not long ago, an urgently needed set of medical instruments was dispatched by aeroplane from London to Dunkirk in three hours.

The representative of a well-known aircraft company, with establishments in London and Paris, frequently makes business trips from one city to the other by way of the air, and usually accomplishes the return journey between early morning and sunset: a record which has been capped by the performance of a "ferry" pilot—taking new machines to, and bringing old machines from, the British Army in France. One summer morning he flew to France and back between breakfast and lunch, had tea in an aerodrome behind the lines, and ended the perfect day by dining at a depot within thirty miles of London. Some feats are even more striking.

There is the possibility of fire. On the comparative safety of land, fire is alarming enough. In the air its terrors are manifold. A pilot is cooped up like a rat in a cage. He cannot dive for the earth—the downward rush would fan up the flames. He cannot take refuge in an inaccessible part of the machine—because there are none. He must sit tight, and hope for the best. Upon one occasion, certainly, an airman did succeed in diving his flaming machine into the sea; but it was by little short of a miracle, and with an after-experience he would not care to repeat. Flying from France to England with a mechanic, six miles from shore the engine of the aeroplane burst into flames. They were at an altitude of over 2,000 feet, but he did not hesitate. The faster they dived, the fiercer grew the flames, the thicker the smoke. Only just in time they plunged into the water.

The 'plane submerged, with the exception of the tip of a wing, and on this they took refuge. Two British destroyers had sighted their descent from a distance. But, just then, a mist blew up. For over an hour the airmen had to wait before being taken off, the machine sinking almost immediately after. Only by his prompt action did the pilot save both their lives.

Promptness is the first essential in flying. Almost out of sight, an aeroplane appears to crawl along the sky-bed. Whereas, in reality, it may be flying at 150 miles an hour. Everything moves in proportion. The mind of the pilot works in tens and scores of miles. His altitude may be varied several thousand feet in a few seconds, by a single touch of the control-stick.

He travels twice as fast as any other human being on land or sea. The latter is similar to the air; but, where it is simple and natural to float in a boat, the aviator is, all the while, forcing the hand of Nature. A grim, protracted struggle with the elements includes the possibility of death by cloud, storm, or "bump" —patch of thin air. Pilots often emerge from clouds unconsciously flying upside down. An observer, sitting two feet in front of the pilot, has had a bullet through his heart, and the latter made his base untouched.

Three times during the war airmen have deliberately driven their machines at an enemy, and hurled down to death, the two locked in flames. An R.A.F. officer, late one afternoon, observed a German "Albatross" swooping low over the British lines, under pretence of dropping a friendly note. Below his fuselage the Britisher caught sight of a camera. He shot him down without hesitation. Aeroplanes have been employed frequently for landing spies inside hostile areas. There was an instance of a young British naval officer circling over a certain fortified area in the South of England, who discovered a man, hidden by a clump of bushes, sketching the harbour from the lee of a hill. He dived for him. But the German spy heard the roar of his engine, and ran off. The airman chased him, and swooping low, shot him down with his machine-gun.

It must be admitted that the German airmen have proved themselves to be as cunning and resourceful as any of their compatriots on the ground. Their finest coup was a recent raid on Paris. In the French capital there is established a series of listening posts, that will detect any aircraft within ten miles. Aware of this fact, a Hun pilot evolved a brilliant strategy. He hovered over the clouds, on the enemy side of the lines, until a French bombing squadron appeared below. He followed it—still out of sight—while they bombed a German ammunition dump; turned south with them, and crossed the lines in their wake.

In order that the noise of his engine should be confounded with that of the French machines, he closed in as near as possible. When the latter sloped down for their aerodrome, the listening posts immediately picked him up. But it was then too late to give warning; and he dashed in over the city, bombing heavily.

Warned by this occurrence, the French took precautions. When the next German squadron arrived over Paris on a night raid, they had the most alarming experience. As one of the pilots participating afterwards wrote in the *Lokal-Anzeiger*:

"Suddenly the French put 'lanterns' in our way. Above and beneath us, ahead and astern, they hung quietly in the air, and with their blinding glare lighted up our 'planes. They are rockets with parachutes provided with very brightly burning fuses. Some special mechanism enables them to remain steady for a full minute in the air. Sometimes dozens together appeared near us to show our machines to the anti-aircraft guns."

The French have rendered finer service to the air than any other nation. They were the first to foster and encourage flying in the early days. Their Air Service is the best organised and equipped of any belligerent. And only when the history of the war comes to be written will the world realise its great debt to Guynemer, Fonck, and their gallant comrades. Here is an instance of the manner in which the French airmen held the fate of Europe for one long, terrible night.

It was about the time of the second Battle of St. Quentin. The

British Fifth Army had gone down before the overwhelming masses of German troops. The latter, by means of rapid and well-organised rail and motor transport, was driving on before the French reserves had time to come up. Behind Arras the enemy had concentrated over a score of "storm" divisions. The country-side was black with troops. The roads were choked with innumerable gun-limbers and ammunition-wagons. Night and day troop-trains puffed up behind the lines; disgorging their cargoes of reinforcements, and puffing away again for more. The fate of Paris hung in the balance.

Then General Petain took action, he told his chief-of-staff:

Order every flying commander within striking distance of Ham, to send up, immediately, every squadron at his disposal—whether fighting or bombing, and concentrate on the German reserves and lines.

Immediately the order was flashed up and down the lines to the French aerodromes. Within half an hour the air was black with machines, all heading for Ham.

All that evening, and through the night that followed, the French airmen swept low over the German masses, bombing and machine-gunning. In seemingly never-ending train, squadron after squadron flew up, loosed off their bombs, used up their ammunition; then returned to their bases for more. The effect was indescribable. The Huns must have been shot down by thousands that night. Booming explosions and columns of flame stabbed the darkness as the ammunition parks went up. The business of bringing up the reserves was abandoned in despair. By the dawn the whole German Army was in state of mad panic. Over two divisions had been put out of action, and their great opportunity lost irretrievably.

This incident must awake even in the most sceptical mind visions of the possibility of aircraft in the future. Those visions will yet be realised when conservative humanity overcomes its hatred of innovation. But, meanwhile, incidental daily events pass unchronicled; events that only go to prove that when man attempted the conquest of the air, he—like Atlas—was taking on something far greater than the exploration of a few continents, or the mastery of five oceans. His unquenchable spirit will always supply the ways; his fertile brain, the means. But he can never wholly overcome the gigantic forces of Nature battling against him.

And even Nature must have turned humorous when she permitted two human beings to fly through the air for over two hours; both of them dead. That is the fact, and this the story. On a clear summer's day three German two-seaters put to air in fighting formation, and chanced upon a solitary British 'plane. Confident in their strength they attacked simultaneously; which was a bad mistake—or this story might never have been told.

The R.A.F. man was quick to profit. Looping sharply overhead, he came down on the back of the rightmost machine—his left—and plugged her. She staggered and dropped from the fight. Her companions waited for no more; but turned for home. The Englishman chased them, firing short bursts from his machine-gun. As he caught sight of the other machine, now 1,000 feet below—at about 5,000 feet over the earth—he thought to finish her off, there and then, and dived for the pilot's back, reserving his fire until within 100 yards. He did so.

When the tray of ammunition had blazed off, the German was still flying as serene as ever. He essayed another burst; but still she flew on a level keel. Again, he fired; again, without result. Then he brought his machine almost within speaking distance, and literally riddled the Hun with bullets. For all his pains, she still swept on, in a circular course, heading for the south.

Curiosity got the better of him, and he followed her close-in for, maybe, half an hour. All the time he fired bursts continually, until his ammunition ran out. By this time, they had been at it for over an hour. But the Britisher held on, determined to see the matter through. Twice they swept across the lines in wide, right-hand circles, averaging over sixty miles apiece. Until, eventually, the stranger machine volplaned down into a field behind the British lines. Both German pilot and observer were dead; killed—unmistakably—by machine-gun bullets. The aeroplane had continued her volition, for almost 200 miles, by inherent stability.

CHAPTER 16

Armageddon From the Skies

An unnameable hero of the British Flying services, bound on "contact patrol," and flying perilously low over the seething battle-field, late one Thursday afternoon, witnessed a sight permitted to few mortal eyes. Whether he appreciated his experience we shall never know. His machine was brought crashing down to earth, and himself killed by an enemy machine-gun before the next day's sunset. His narrative, however, will be handed down to history. He was flying somewhere north-west of St. Quentin. Here is the extract from the letter:

> Since an early hour in the afternoon, rolling clouds of picric smoke smothered the surface of the earth, almost obscuring it from reconnaissance. The effect was most startling. At one moment, the mirage would roll back like a coverlet; the stretch of road and railway, village and field below, would be almost bare of movement. At another, through a rift could be caught a fleeting glimpse of indescribable masses of grey, which at first against the greyer shadow of the earth would appear motionless, then develop animation at numerous points; a great human snake that writhed this way and that, endeavouring to free itself from its own voluminous coils. I dived lower, and rapidly fired off a tray and a half of cartridges from my machine-gun, encountering little or no defensive fire, and certainly causing casualties.
>
> A broad, straight highway, running directly north and south, indicated Le V——, where a great mass of British infantry the Umpth Division—was lying. Gradually, very gradually, it was dwindling away in long, ceaseless tendrils from the main body, to a more expansive mass in the rear-ground. Tiny shoots of flame stabbed the smoke cloud from all directions. It was denser here, and difficult to distinguish friend from foe. . . . The hurl

and shock and recoil of the infantry battle were here plainly visible. . ... By this time, I had run out of ammunition. So, I flew off westward, through the smoke, to the clearer atmosphere beyond, leaving the charred, smouldering carnage of what had once been a pleasant countryside of rolling meadows and woodlands behind me with a feeling of repugnance.

For almost a fortnight, British and German aeroplanes had been disputing the airway over the theatre of future operations. Sir Douglas Haig by March 14th had received information of the coming Push from the Intelligence branch of the Flying Corps; to whom a reconnaissance patrol pilot had reported that "the enemy were carrying out intensive training with tanks, sixty miles behind their lines." Other reports spoke of congestion on roads and railways, particularly in the Courtrai, Lille, Douai, Valenciennes, Mons, Cambrai, and Hirson districts. And it was common knowledge that the enemy had carried through a great lay-out of railway track in the region of the Meuse, shortening by fifty miles all communication between the internal industrial centres and the dumps and supply bases immediately in rear of the firing line.

The aerial fighting which immediately preceded the battle was the fiercest in history. Day after day, huge British bombing 'planes flew over Mannheim, and other large military centres and railway junctions; blowing up railway sidings, aeroplane sheds, and munition dumps, from low altitudes. From the first tinge of dawn to the last moment of twilight, photography, reconnaissance, and artillery-directing aeroplanes were hovering over their lines. All through the day and far into the night, at higher altitudes above the racing clouds, British and German machines met in Homeric combat, endeavouring to gain the mastery in that particular sector.

Then came the first actual raid of the battle. On the fifteenth, R.F.C. pilots bombed the railway sidings at Hirson, which were congested with troop and ammunition trains waiting to proceed to the battle, causing considerable damage to rolling stock and permanent way. And, ten hours later, under cover of the darkness, the barracks, munition factories, and the railway station of Zweibrucken were subjected to a destructive bombing.

From that time until the dawn of the eighteenth, aerial activity continued without cessation. A large concentration of German infantry, waiting at Kaiserlautern before being flung into the battle line, were literally mown down with bombs and machine-gun fire. In one single night raid a further sixty tons of bombs were dropped on two German aerodromes, which were the bases for the German night-flying machines. Then, on the nineteenth, came an ominous lull; due to rain and clouds, which continued until late into the evening of the twentieth. During this period, however, an extensive bomb raid was carried out on a large shell depot north-east of St. Quentin, which only that morning—according to an Allied spy, who had been dropped three days before in the German lines, and picked up after twilight of the twentieth—had been stocked roof high with shells for the coming battle.

By this time all that was humanly possible had been done to meet the coming offensive. The British Army and the Flying Corps in particular were ready at every point, and awaited the event with calm deliberation. Those who could read between the lines of the official *communiqués* realised that the long-advertised Push was imminent. With Thursday's renewed and desperate aerial activity, this realisation waxed a certainty. Away up in the North Sea, in the Bight of Heligoland, British seaplanes were patrolling constantly, watching for any attempt on the enemy's side of a concerted movement on the part of his fleet.

The mist of Thursday morning cleared towards midday, but only in certain localities. In most places the light was only suitable for low flying. Nevertheless, the British airmen succeeded in locating great bodies of enemy reinforcements, and pouring many thousands of rounds into them, causing innumerable casualties. At first the antiaircraft defences were unusually violent. Then the Germans, apparently with the idea that any further attempt at concealment was useless, ceased fire, or kept up only a pretence. The bombing machines dropped no fewer than 900 bombs on railway stations immediately behind the lines, causing the enemy reinforcements and supplies of ammunition a delay of at least twelve hours.

Even at the low altitude at which flying was possible on this day, the air fighting was tremendous. Sixteen Hun aeroplanes were brought down, and six driven down. One of these was flying so low as to be shot down by British infantry within their own lines. Bombs were dropped on further large bodies of German reinforcements, rather to the north-west of Tournai. And here for the next twenty-four hours— and many twenty-four afterwards—all aerial activity was centred.

Came the night before the battle. At sundown, clouds and mist hung low over the face of the sky. Behind the mist, beneath the low clouds, a few miles to the west was the incessant *jog-jog-jog* of armed men; on high roads, and by-roads, across the fields, and by the railway tracks. But the Flying Corps missed nothing of all these preparations. Whenever there came a break, a reconnaissance machine would go speeding westwards. An hour later the pilot would return, the observer with a bulky report. From another aerodrome, farther down the line, other machines would go out, and other machines return with fresh enemy dispositions, fresh enemy ammunition dumps, fresh enemy gun positions; here a concentration of tanks, there a railway being run up to the trenches.

The fight was grim and merciless, from the moment they left the ground until they came winging home again, with perhaps a broken strut, or a wing barely hinging on the supports, and sometimes with the pilot or the observer mortally wounded. The enemy were determined they should not gain information. They were out to get it at all costs. The staff alone knew the result of this long unequal combat; and they benefited thereby, to a very considerable degree. As observer after observer handed in fresh returns, the wires got busy behind the British lines, half-way across the North of France, calling for reinforcements from all parts.

Through the long night of waiting, and in the teeth of the storm and gales, every available night-flying squadron in the battle area was turned out into the skies. Haig himself reports that:

> Our bombing squadrons dropped 300 bombs alone on a hostile aerodrome south-west of Tournai, used by the enemy's night-flying squadrons, and also on a large ammunition depot north-east of St. Quentin.

At the dawn, with the mist still hanging over the surface of the ground—almost like a sea fog, before the pallid grey light broke through the faint glimmer of the sinking moon—the R.F.C. had carried out a score and one reconnaissances. They had seen the great masses waiting, grimly silent, behind the enemy trenches; they had seen the gleaming muzzles of the giant howitzers and smaller field guns in every hole and corner. The story of their report sheets, when—and if ever—it is written, will beggar credulity. Towards the dawn a terrific artillery bombardment opened by the enemy's guns. Shortly after a pilot landed at an aerodrome behind the British positions—barely beyond shellfire; frightened, white countenanced, but yet unafraid, he managed to blurt out: "There are thousands of them—thousands! The whole countryside is alive with advancing infantry." Then they came racing across the devastated patch of No Man's Land.

From all corners of the heavens, British airmen came swooping down on to them like avenging angels, firing and bombing as they dived. But the Germans appeared to ignore them. Men fell on all sides. Still they marched on. No power on earth could have stopped that living tide! Back went the airmen for more ammunition. Down they swooped through the mist again. Still the enemy came marching on. Shattered for all time was the theory that aircraft would be the deciding factor in modern war. But they demonstrated most admirably that they could hold up reinforcements until either the enemy rushed up a battery of machine guns, or the 'plane fell to earth, a shattered wreck.

When the enemy endeavoured to snatch a brief rest that night, they were at them again, bombing and killing. Three and a half tons of bombs they dropped on villages and camps to the north-west of Tournai.

This, however, gave the Hun his cue. At daybreak the following morning, his aeroplanes swooped up from all sides the low-flying machines being particularly active, engaging our forward troops with their machine-guns. The only fault to find with our own pilots was perhaps that they did not take the affair with the due seriousness which it warranted. But that is not the English spirit. They go languidly to their pleasures, laughingly to their deaths. They were not languid this morning.

Between Arras and St. Quentin, the main aerial combat raged. The mastery of the battle area fluctuated; now to one side, now to the other. Eventually the British had it. Day for day, night for night, these conditions were repeated, until at last the Allied Army stood firm and unshakable behind the line of the old Somme battlefield. The adventures of the airmen, meanwhile, ran through the gamut of the emotions. One night the low-flying pilots came home and reported that the ground immediately behind the enemy advance was strewn for miles with grey corpses. Another afternoon a reconnaissance pilot—plaintively enough—described having seen a great army of Huns, all plunging into the battle in brand-new uniforms. As one of them commented: "Imagine they are going to dine in Paris tonight!"

At low altitudes the German airmen appeared to adapt their reconnaissance to the policy of peep and run. Immediately the skyline showed clear, they would come flying over. Then a British machine appeared, and they turned for home as fast as they could go. But, up high, a bombing squadron sped away, destined for Paris. The French, however, were prepared for them, and, after a desultory attempt, they dropped their bombs on Compiegne, and returned again.

Saturday the 23rd was remarkable for the bombardment of Paris by the—now famous—German heavy gun. Hostile aeroplanes over the city in the early morning hours heralded the commencement of this manoeuvre. At first they were thought to be bomb raiders. But as they kept to a very great altitude, and circled continually without dropping any bombs, it soon became obvious that their intention was to direct the gunfire. Back at the firing lines, Haig reported:

> Many thousands of rounds fired from a low height on hostile troops massed in villages and in the open. Bombing carried out continuously all the day. Over fourteen tons of bombs dropped on enemy's billets, high-velocity guns—which presumably included the Paris gun—and stations in battle area.

Later the same day it was reported:

> Our machines carried out another most successful raid on factories at Mannheim. Nearly a ton and a half of bombs was dropped and bursts were seen on the (Badische) soda factory (great chemical works) and railway and on the docks. Several fires were started, one of which was of great size, with flames reaching to a height of 200 feet and smoke to 5,000 feet. Fire visible for thirty-five miles.

Another day over 1,700 tons of bombs were dropped on varying targets, which included enemy docks, stations, camps, high-velocity guns and reinforcements. This day was notable as being the heaviest in the course of the whole battle. Forty-five German aeroplanes were brought down, and twenty-two driven down out of control. After this enemy craft were conspicuous by their absence for miles around; whereas British machines came flocking over the battlefield in ever-increasing numbers.

"A total of twenty-two tons of bombs were dropped by us, and over 100,000 rounds were fired from machine-guns," was the welcome news contained in the following day's Official; on receipt of which the Air Board dispatched the following telegram to General Salmond, the young commander of the Flying Corps in the field:

> The Air Council congratulate you and all ranks of the R.N.A.S., R.F.C., and Australian Flying Corps on the splendid work car-

ried out during this great battle. We are all following their great deeds, and know that they will keep it going.

And to which he returned his famous message:

Very many thanks for Air Council's congratulations, which are much appreciated by all concerned. All ranks have their tails well up, and the superiority of British over enemy airmen has never been more marked.

On the 26th the enemy issued his resume of aerial fighting for the whole battle:

Since the beginning of the battle ninety-three enemy aeroplanes and six captive balloons have been brought down. Cavalry Captain Baron von Richthofen achieved his 67th and 68th aerial victories.

Comparing this with Haig's daily reports, it shows a considerable advantage on our side. Thus, in five days, March 21st-25th inclusive:

German aeroplanes destroyed or captured		137
Driven down out of control	83	
Balloons destroyed		3
Total		223

As an appreciation of this unequalled performance, King George sent the following telegram to Sir Douglas Haig:

I wish to express to General Salmond and all ranks of the Air Services of the British Empire in France my gratification at their splendid achievements during this great battle. I am proud to be their Colonel-in-Chief.

Thus ends the first chapter of the Flying Services as an army of combat. What they proved capable of in those few strenuous days will alter materially all military theories of strategy and tactics of the future. In that period, they put up many fine achievements, but none finer than that reported by Reuter's special correspondent on the 27th. Thus:

Two entire German divisions advancing towards the battle front were almost completely annihilated, before they were able to fire a single shot, by machine-gun fire and bombs from about a hundred French aeroplanes.

CHAPTER 17

The Aerial Duel—And Aerial Duellists

"Good duellist, bad soldier," asserted the great Napoleon. But he was wrong. The aerial duellists of the twentieth century, Ball and Bishop, Guynemer, McCudden, and Richthofen, were to give the lie to his assertion. The "Iron Duke," who hammered him at Waterloo, knew better. "A little duelling now and then doesn't hurt the Hussars," he said, when consulted by the Prince Regent about punishments. He had been out himself.

Caesar's legions regarded with contempt the German judicial belayings, in Teutonic forests, 2,000 years ago. An Italian noblewoman, a century later, complained of the call of a gentleman, after hours, as a blazing indiscretion. They put a sword into his hand, and set a bravo on to him. He did not survive, to benefit by the confession of that rascally sneak who had imposed upon the lady. Duelling was unfashionable in that particular city for years afterward. Boulanger was foolish enough to get himself pinked by an ordinary fellow, thus losing his chance of becoming another Napoleon. In his brilliant comedy, *The Rivals*, Sheridan made duelling a matter of festive sport; while, only last year, Sir Douglas Haig dispatched to Britain's greatest aerial duellist a personal note, "Well done. D. H."

In 1600 it was plainly ridiculous; in 1900-odd it seems almost knightly. Many a fine fellow has been sent by kings and cardinals to the gibbet because of it. Popes have levelled the terrors of hell against it. Court-martialled and cashiered, good officers have ended in the gutter because they would play at it. Since the days of Louis XIV civilisation has labelled it murder. Only laughter could exterminate the wager of battle. Modern conditions, modern necessities have mocked at laughter. Duelling has again become an honourable and heroic thing in the eyes of men. These Homeric combats of the English or the French against the Germans, in the highway of the air, are not styled duels; but nevertheless, that is what they are.

The aerial combat grips the imagination with a force that no other sensation can provide. It is the gauntlet of man's progressiveness flung into the face of the elements. Two miles aloft, barely distinguishable against the glare of the sky and the enveloping mists of the clouds, there creep up two waspish, attenuated shapes—apparently from the ends of the horizon. A sudden burst of sunshine finds them as they wheel into the fight. It plays along the glistening wings, radiating from a thousand different points; now at the burnished engine fittings at the nose, now the struts of the wings apparent against the blue. One is above, and a little behind. He streaks for his opponent's tail. So near, that from the ground it appears inevitable they must collide, and crash, helplessly wrecked, to the earth. Gradually the two forms dissemble themselves, and again spring into action; wheeling, tumbling, with delightful recklessness, skimming each other, by inches, at a break-neck speed, twisting, climbing, diving, up and down every chord of the heavens.

To the infantry and gunners watching anxiously below, it is the grandest spectacle of the war. They envy the daring airmen with all their hearts. To them the affair possesses a curiously personal aspect. It is their fight. There, in their trenches, and behind their guns, they experience every dive and twist, and turn, with a vividness that is remarkable. And when at last one or the other makes his last dip down that tortuous stair of flight, a tense expectancy prevails—until either the black crosses or the circles of red, white, and blue become visible on the vanquished craft. If it is the one, the air is rent with deep-throated cheers; if the other, a murmur goes down the line of British trenches like the moan of the wind through the trees.

That is how Guynemer died. A month later Guynemer's friend met his vanquisher; destroying him, in kind. And what was Guynemer but another D'Artagnan? Ball of the Flying Corps was another Athos; Richthofen a Teuton De Wardes. Over Cambrai and Picardy and Waterloo they refought the fatal encounters of their ancestors. One century came Wellington, with horse and foot; the next Bishop goes winging across the Flanders plains, in a frail aeroplane. It is the modern expression of the ineradicable thirst of men for personal combat.

The most savage duellist of the war, Boelke, whose letters to his parents proved him to be without mercy or compassion, died at the duel. Captain Ball, our great "ace," was brought down by a Hun star who had shadowed him for months. The Allies do not recognise these combats of individuals officially; but the enemy makes use of the exploits of her great flying men for propaganda purposes in her own and neutral countries. More famous of these so-styled champions are Baron von Richthofen, with sixty-four allied machines to his credit; Werner Moss of Crefeld, with forty-seven; the notorious Boelke, with forty; Lieutenant Wolf, with thirty-three; and Lieutenant Schafer, with thirty. Immelmann had brought down twenty-eight Allied aeroplanes before himself being destroyed by a British battleplane.

Comparing these totals—which it may be mentioned include captive balloons, that our airmen never take into account with those of the crack French and British pilots, the balance is easily on our side. Here is a brief summary:

Captain McCudden, R.F.C.	57	
Captain Ball, V.C.		53
Capt. Georges Guynemer		51
Captain Bishop, V.C.	47	

Every one of these great fighters has developed his own methods of attack. There was no precedent to fall back on. Warneford was the first of the British duellists. He attacked, in a tiny monoplane, a giant Zeppelin twenty times his size. It was a repetition of David slaying Goliath. His official award of the Victoria Cross was announced as:

"For destroying single-handed a German Zeppelin. Afterwards, although forced to descend on enemy soil, he succeeded in flying back safely."

Ball was the "Scarlet Pimpernel" of the skies. He would wait above the clouds, at a great altitude, watching the enemy aerodromes. Immediately a German aeroplane would attempt to take the air, he would dive for it and drive it to earth again. Somewhere below, British craft would be attacked in overwhelming numbers. Again, he would swoop down on top of them, putting them to flight.

In direct opposition to this code were the methods of the Hun, Boelke. Of forty air fights in which the latter participated, it is said that ten were duels with men he had challenged or been challenged by. Because his antagonists played the game, he escaped from more than one encounter which should have gone against him. Boelke had no use for the rules of chivalry.

His plan was never to take any risks, but to allow our pilots to assume the offensive. And, in support of this theory, he once informed a German newspaper man:

It has been said that the German airmen never fly over hostile lines, and that they always remain over territory occupied by their own troops. As regards chasing machines, that is true; but it should be remembered, firstly, that our new machines have some features which we ought to keep to ourselves, and, secondly, that our object is only to prevent hostile aeroplanes from carrying out their observations. It is for these reasons that we prefer to wait for them where we expect to meet them.

Another method was that of the late Lieutenant Immelmann, who would follow an enemy machine from a great altitude, keeping above him all the time. Then, when a favourable opportunity presented itself, dive straight for his tail, firing at him until he was in close proximity. If the manoeuvre were unsuccessful, he would cover his own retreat by continuing the dive and coming out in a semi-circular direction.

While von Richthofen, on the other hand, always hunts with a small squadron at his command. They fly in two lines. Above is the leader, alone. Three other craft are below. Immediately an Allied machine is sighted, Richthofen climbs above the clouds, while his consorts endeavour to surround the hostile craft. When this has been accomplished successfully, he dives straight at the Allied machine, using his machine-gun all the while.

A year or so before the war an Englishman and his wife were sitting in one of the most famous beer gardens in Berlin, when a Prussian officer commenced to ogle her. Annoyed with this unmannerly conduct, the Englishman went over and remonstrated with him. The interview terminated with the Prussian getting a smart clout across the head. There was a great flurry and to-do, but for political reasons a duel was made impossible and the Englishman returned to his own home.

When the war broke out the Prussian learnt that his adversary had become an officer in the Flying Services, He managed to get himself transferred to aviation, moved by the one obsessive thought of finding that Englishman some day and killing him.

Two years went by, and he came no nearer to his ambition; but it was observed that the Prussian before attacking an Ally machine invariably took extra risks by flying close and by taking time to scrutinise carefully the features of the enemy pilot. He killed, when he could, without heat. Until at last they met one summer's day, somewhere down there, over the Somme. They say the fight was one to remember. It went on without a break, for over an hour. And both were killed.

Sometimes it is a matter of military policy to seek out and destroy individuals, each as dangerous as an army corps. Thus, a sort of splendid jealousy develops. Richthofen resents the greatness of Bishop. It becomes his or another German's obsession to find and kill this troublesome rival. In one phrase you have the ethics of aerial combat.

Georges Guynemer soared one morning to seek a certain German who had annoyed him. The story is told by an R.F.C. officer, in a letter home.

> He and another officer went out on Tuesday morning to hunt the Hun. They were flying fairly high, somewhere around 16,000 feet, I think, and Guynemer went down a little way to attack a biplane, while the lieutenant who was with him stayed up to protect his rear.
>
> About that time eight Boche monoplanes put in an appearance, and the lieutenant was kept busy trying to worry them and keep them from going down to the captain. He succeeded, and none of the Boches dived down, but in the general mix-up he lost track of Guynemer and he has not been heard from since. The loss of this man is very great, as he was by all odds the greatest aviator and individual fighter the war has produced.
>
> As I have already written you, he was very small and of frail appearance. I believe his health was very far from good, and the high altitudes sometimes made him so sick he had to come down. He would fly for a week, then go away for a rest, as he was not strong enough to stand any more.
>
> In the course of several hundred fights he has been shot down seven times and twice wounded. To keep at it under such circumstances and after all he had gone through, a man's heart has to be in the right place. He certainly deserved to live the rest of his days in peace, and one hates to see a man like that get it. Long immunity breeds a contempt of danger, which is probably the greatest danger of all.

All the world knows, Guynemer was killed fighting. His body was found by a sergeant of German infantry, lying by the roadside with his battered machine. The Germans afterwards erected a monument over the spot.

Again, this officer wrote:

> One of our cracks got square the other day with the man who

is reported to have killed Guynemer. This German was a captain and an observer in a biplane. The observer is the man who handles the movable machine-gun in a biplane.

The Boche machine had flown from far behind their lines to take pictures, but was very high, over 20,000 feet, probably relying largely upon his height for protection, for an ordinary fighting plane will not go that high. Our man, who is very expert and who has been a pilot for a long time, was in a particularly powerful machine, and was the only one who saw the Boche who could get up to him.

He climbed up under and behind his tail. Every time the Boche pilot would try to turn in order to give his gunner a shot, the Frenchman would slide around also, always keeping the Hun's own tail between himself and the machine-gunner, so that the latter could not shoot without shooting away his own controls. In this manner he got right on top of the Boche, and at the first salvo put his machine-gun out of business and probably hit the gunner—that is, the captain who is supposed to have shot Guynemer. After that there was nothing to it. The second dose the Frenchman gave him cut away the supports of the wings on one side so that they came out of position. The Hun flopped over on his back and Guynemer's supposed slayer fell out of his machine, taking a nice little tumble of 20,000 feet.

The machine and pilot tumbled end over end, and as they went by a number of French machines waiting below, who had not been able to get up, amused themselves by taking pot shots at them.

It is one story but typical of many. Bishop has again returned to France after a well-earned rest. McCudden was a youth of twenty-three, who joined the army, eight years ago, as a private; transferred to the Flying Corps in 1912; where he was promoted to captain, as a reward for some of the most brilliant flying work of the war. His total bag numbered fifty-seven Hun machines, nine of which he brought down in a fortnight, the remainder including forty-seven two-seated Boches. Achilles pursuing Hector around the walls of Troy is simply Bishop seeking Richthofen among the clouds.

CHAPTER 18

Sawbone Soliloquies

The perfect airman; who is he? What are those especial qualifications that so harden him to those unexpected dangers and nerve-trying moments of flying? At what exact age is he at his flying "prime"? What are his characteristics? Should he be tall or short; light or heavy? Is good eyesight or hearing essential? Which is to repeat but a few of the queries that are crowding the flying aspirant's mind, now that our aerial cavalry are so much to the forefront of the great battle.

Opinions on this matter vary to a considerable degree. Only recently a British Member of Parliament called attention to the need for more efficient medical supervision in the training of our airmen. This, he explained, was essential by reason of the dangerous effect of high altitudes on very young men. And immediately afterwards a well-known flying commander traversed his opinion with the statement that "beginners were never taken up to high altitudes until they had had considerable experience in flying."

But the medico M.P.'s views were supplemented by the letter of another officer of the R.A.M.C. to *The Evening Standard*:

Man is an animal intended by Nature to live on a ground level. In an aeroplane he can rapidly ascend 10,000 or 20,000 feet, and even more rapidly descend.

During both the ascent and descent, the surface of the body is subject to very rapid changes of pressure; and unsuspected weak spots are disclosed and peculiar deviations from health observed.

A comparable condition is observed in divers and other persons who have to work under high air pressures. When these persons are relieved too suddenly of the pressure under which they have been working, as may easily arise in the case of a forced ascent from deep water or a too rapid decompression in an air-lock, a train of symptoms is produced which is known as 'Caisson Disease,' having its converse parallel in the case of an airman making a rapid descent from a high altitude.

This correspondent states that he was surprised at the flight-commander's statement that airmen do not care a button whether they are flying at 1,0,000 or 6,000 feet.

Men faint at high altitudes and experience great difficulty in breathing, who on the ground show no sign of trouble except to a scientific eye. It is simply courting disaster to attempt to 'fit by slow degrees' such men to such work. How many beginners crashed under instruction, before the scientist laid down the standards now universally employed?

That perfect vision was the first essential of the perfect airman was the agreement of many prominent medical men and flyers, who recently held a meeting at the Medical Society of London to discuss this subject.

The principal speaker was a young naval surgeon—an ex-Harley-Street specialist—Surgeon Graeme Anderson, who had had considerable experience in examining airmen since the beginning of the war, and also holds a flying pilot's certificate. He related how, upon a certain occasion, he made an experiment by going up as a passenger with his ears plugged and his eyes blindfolded.

I wanted to find out if I could tell the movements of the machine without seeing or hearing. After a while we seemed to be going up and up, on an almost even keel, but as a matter of fact we were descending. . . . Only men almost perfect from the physical point of view should be allowed to fly, and even those accepted should be graded for flying at different heights and then for different duties.

Men who suffer from chilblains should be passed only for low flying, because chilblains are an indication that they are not medically fit to rise to great altitudes.

He deprecated the taking of alcohol by pilots.

The action of a little alcohol is intensified greatly by flying, and while I have known men do some amazing 'stunts' under its influence, it always beats them in the end. A man of this kind retained on one of his worst days a power of reasoning which, in spite of sleepiness, made him decide not to attempt any 'stunts.' So he set off for home—thirty miles away. Over his aerodrome he performed almost unheard-of antics. Ultimately he 'crashed,' and when he recovered consciousness he said that until the last moment he could remember he had stuck to his resolve not to do 'stunts.' The perfect age for flying is twenty-four.

And later, Surgeon Anderson supplemented his views with an article in *The Illustrated Sunday Herald,* as follows:

Scarcely ten years ago the pioneer aviators were looked upon as men possessing some supernatural quality—the power to fly. All that is now changed.

Man began to teach man, and the institution of the dual-control methods of instruction, in which teacher and pupil fly in the same aeroplane, each with a set of controls acting in unison, paved the way for many to learn flying.

Hundreds of young Britons are now passing straight from the school to the aerodrome, and from the aerodrome to the flying front.

It is well to know something of the aviator's duties in wartime. For the most part, he has unusually comfortable quarters, a good bed and food, and has not to undergo the long marches and discomforts of trench life as in infantry work.

He is usually out of range of enemy artillery fire, although subject to hostile aircraft attack. In bad flying weather he has much leisure time. On the other hand, in the few crowded hours of his daily work he may come through the most intense strain to which the human nervous system can be subjected.

As it has been aptly put, an aviator's life consists of 'long spells of idleness, punctuated by moments of intense fear.' He has to face extremes in the elements—intense cold, the sun's glare, rain, wind, fog, and misty and gusty or bumpy weather.

There is the incessant noise of the engine—he may have long-distance patrols, in which the imagination is given free play to run riot, perhaps over the sea, with no landmarks and the dread of engine failure ever present in his mind.

His visual acuteness is sharpened, always on the look-out for hostile aircraft, watching for and registering the flash of enemy guns, taking photographs, noting movements of enemy troops, rolling stock, submarines, or other information of naval or military value, and subjected to more or less accurate antiaircraft gunfire from the ground.

Often, he has to reach altitudes where the available oxygen is reduced by one-half. He may have constantly and rapidly to change height, as in the modern aerial fighting, he may be opposing more than one enemy machine. His judgment has to be most accurate to perform the various intricate aerial evolutions so as to outwit his opponent and gain a favourable position to rake him with machine-gun fire.

He may have to loop, spin, dive, or sideslip apparently out of control, in order to deceive or to decoy his opponent over a friendly gun or near a friendly formation.

There is the subconscious dread of his aeroplane catching fire in the air, and lastly, and most exciting of all, the nerve-strain of contour chasing or ground strafing in which he attacks the enemy on the ground from a low height of perhaps twenty feet to fifty feet.

For the past three and a half years I have lived with aviators, flown with them, and entered for the most part into their interests, studying them alike in squadrons, in aeroplane, seaplane, and airship stations, and in hospitals specially devoted to their maladies.

Let me here pay a tribute to our flying men, 'that nothing is too good for them, and it is up to us as a profession to strive in every way we can to safeguard them from disease, and should disease overtake them, to find the means to restore them to health again.'

We can help in this matter by knowing the requirements of the aviator's life, by studying the psychology and physiology of flying, and by investigating the maladies commonly found amongst flying men.

In eliminating the unfit, and as manpower is an ever-increasing problem, I would suggest the institution of a special flying school where 'border-line' pupils could be instructed in flying under patient and sympathetic instructors, and with a medical officer specially interested in aviation carefully recording the results.

Such records would be invaluable to us in confirming or modifying the present standards of fitness required for air work.

The modern aviator's work is becoming more and more specialised, and here again we can help by framing standards of fitness graded by the various flying duties.

In selecting candidates for the Air Service, what is looked for is a sound constitution, free from organic disease, and a fairly strong physique in order to withstand altitude effects, such as cold, fatigue, and diminished oxygen. It is essential that there should be normal hearing and good muscle and equilibration sense.

As the aviator is so much dependent on his eyesight, too much importance cannot be laid on this part of the examination. But next to vision, and most important of all in obtaining the best aviator, is the question of temperament.

Undoubtedly there is a particular temperament or aptitude for flying, and its distribution is particularly interesting, whether looked upon from its racial aspect or its relation to health, life, and habits. Unfortunately, this temperament is a difficult matter to estimate clinically, and especially so in the examining room.

The ideal aviator must have good judgment, be courageous, and not upset by fear, although conscious of the perils of his work. He must be cool in emergencies, able to make careful and quick decisions, and act accordingly. His reaction times must never be delayed; he must be ever alert, as mental sluggishness in flying spells disaster.

Whether he should be imaginative or not is a difficult question to settle—one meets many of both types. I am inclined to think that the pilot with imagination, yet able to keep it well under control, makes the better pilot.

With regard to the relation of habits in this special aptitude for flying, it is found most commonly amongst those used to playing games and leading an outdoor life. The yachtsman and the horseman, with their fine sense of judgment and 'lighter hands,' should make the most skilful pilots.

The Germans always selected their aviators from their cavalry until recently. It was thought that racing motorists would make the best pilots, but this has not been proved to be the case.

Every now and again one meets a type with splendid physique and apparently unshakable courage who learns to fly indifferently or is unable to learn at all, and again one meets the weedy, pale type learning to fly quickly and turning out to be a first-rate pilot.

In the surgical examination the age, height, weight, and general physique are considered. The age should be between eighteen and thirty. Under eighteen and up to twenty, caution and well-balanced judgment may be lacking; twenty-four is about the best age; and over thirty-three the candidate, although quite able to learn to fly, does not stand the nerve strain of air work so well. Cody learned to fly at forty-seven, and was flying regularly till he met his death when fifty-two years of age.

Naturally, the lighter the candidate the better, but in modern times, with the increased speed and climb of aeroplanes, this does not count so much as formerly.

As a general rule, those whose previous occupation has been of an outdoor nature, and those who have been accustomed to playing outdoor games, make the better aviators although, as in most things, the exceptions to the rule are to be found in the thoughtful, quiet, student type who rarely play any games, yet surprise everyone by their rapidity in learning to fly, and in developing 'light hands,' and conversely we meet the type who learn to fly without difficulty, and develop hands like hams as far as piloting an aeroplane is concerned.

An inquiry is made into the candidate's habits, especially in relation to tobacco and alcohol, although very little real knowledge is gained in the examining room. Most flying men smoke a great deal, and very few are strict teetotallers.

I firmly believe that to the aviator excess in alcohol will ultimately beat him. And it is obvious that defective eyesight or colour vision or imperfect hearing may lead a pilot to death.

Chapter 19

L'Envoi

O. Henry, quietly ambling through life, plumbing the depths of Humanity's being; Mr. Britling, that all-wise philosopher, sitting by his night-desk at quiet Dunmow, alternately watching and wondering at the great world run riot, careering around him with a chaos of conflicting emotions—may have penned a similar story, and—with the grey dawn—consigned it to his capacious wastebasket as insufficient—lacking in reality and local colour.

It was for some unknown Belgian woman—untricked in the craft of letters—to present that one story of the air to a breathless world. It was only a matter of a few lines, but its spirit was that of nineteen long centuries of men and heroes; Empire builders all. She enclosed it with a snapshot of a shattered British aeroplane, a pitiful heap of smouldering ashes and distorted metal, and she wrote:

> What a pity such heroes should have to die! They could have escaped, but preferred to fight to a finish. Never have I seen such gallant resistance before. . . . The two heroes were buried with military honour.

The scene flashes away again. It has all the rapid changing and many-sided phases of the realm of sky they serve. This time there is a haunting memory of some epic of the past; a suggestion of the muffled roll of drums for some doughty old warrior of the Peninsular Wars. But this is more poignant in its sorrow, more simple in its execution. "If any music is played at my funeral," he had demanded, somewhat whimsically—proud in the strength of his buoyant youth—"let it be the 'March of the Men of Harlech.'" Ten days later, he had flown west to the Valhalla of the airman, beyond the racing clouds; an almost unrecognisable figure, blackened and disfigured by the sudden hell of flaming petrol, as his 'plane plunged headlong for the earth.

As I piece together these so-varied stories, often the thought comes flashing into my mind, "Could Dumas and Swift have somehow come together in that great world beyond, and collaborated; these their joint effusions?" But they could never have supplied the climax. Edgar Allen Poe must have had a hand in that. And even his wizardry stands me in poor stead, when I remember the tragic scene of which I was an unwilling spectator, now some two years ago.

It was at sunset; one of those red-gold sunsets of Kent. The broad sweep of green aerodrome and the broader sweep of blue sky beyond were alive with darting aircraft, "upstairs" for the last time before nightfall. One by one, they came slithering home again, until but one remained.

How, when, or why exactly it happened, none can say. But as this last 'plane came nosing down to the landing-ground, another craft from the far end rushed up into the air. Too late they tried to warn him. At a height of just over the level of the shed-roofs the two machines crashed into one another. There was a sudden unnerving jar, that seemed to echo across the quiet fields for miles around; a tearing and a rending, as of a thousand rushing wings, and a second later two ugly heaps lay in adjacent fields.

There was a pilot and an observer in one, and a pilot in the other machine, a fighting scout. All were dead!

Bad luck, you may call it, or maybe fate. But there is an unbelievable element of the sway of that capricious little god where flying is concerned. Ask any airman of your acquaintance, or take note of the following:

Flying—to be more correct, 'getting off' from the ground, and when still at a height of only between 200 and 300 feet above the surface—the engine of a 'plane went off dead. Down she came, almost in a 'nosedive,' and struck a tree with her wing, whirling round and round.

In the air the human mind moves rapidly. In the brief space of time that had been permitted him, the pilot, seeing his danger, had unclasped his belt and leapt out, escaping with nothing more than a shaking. His machine meanwhile had dashed to the ground and turned turtle. Had he remained in her, he would have been killed.

Erwin Haertl was a Hun; but for that, a sportsman and a man. He died from wounds behind his own lines after having, a few minutes before, at 9,000 feet in the air, brought down a British pilot. Half-way through the fight he was mortally wounded, but nevertheless stuck it to the end—though he had to stand up in his machine, and knew that it meant certain death to do so.

Rudyard Kipling must have taken that story to his heart. And how he must have revelled in that other reported by the war correspondent of the *Petit Parisien*, that went:

> We were passing through the Lozière Wood, west of Ailly-sur-Noye, when a British aeroplane fell down 300 metres away from us. The motor caught fire, and in a moment the machine was enveloped in flames. In the furnace, strapped to his seat and motionless, was the pilot, a very young officer, almost a lad. His head reclined on his shoulder, and in his pale face the half-closed eyes gave no sign of life. But he was still alive, and when consciousness returned, he showed great surprise at finding himself in the house where he had been immediately conveyed. In what a terrible drama had this unfortunate lad played during the space of but a few minutes!
>
> He had been on a reconnoitring trip and was flying very low to spy the enemy's positions, when eight German aeroplanes dashed at him. He rose immediately, simulated flight, and then by splendid manoeuvring sent three of the enemy spinning to earth. At that moment he felt a sharp pain in the head. A machine-gun bullet had struck him. Others whistled by his ears, and a second broke his collarbone. His head swam, and the buzzing of the engines deafened all sound.
>
> Yet a third bullet tore through the young officer's neck, and three more struck him in various parts of the body. He could do no more, and shot for earth. Though bleeding from many wounds and hardly able to hold up his head, he still retained enough command over the machine to avoid capsizing it, and so came to ground.

But perhaps the most poignant incident of all was when Sergeant Thomas Mottershead of the old R.F.C. went up to his death. True, he was awarded a posthumous V.C. But what was the Bronze Cross in comparison to such a deed?

At 9,000 feet he was set upon and outnumbered by Hun machines. Fighting gallantly, one of the enemy bullets pierced the petrol-tank of his 'plane, and immediately it caught fire.

Enveloped in flames, which his observer, Lieutenant Gower,

was unable to subdue, this very gallant soldier succeeded in bringing his aeroplane back to our lines; and though he made a successful landing, the machine collapsed on touching the ground, pinning him beneath the wreckage, from which he was subsequently rescued. Though suffering extreme torture from burns, Sergeant Mottershead showed the most conspicuous presence of mind in the careful selection of a landing-place, and his wonderful endurance and fortitude undoubtedly saved the life of his observer. He has since died from his wounds.

And so, to the end. Jules Verne must have taken part in this great flight; if not in person, at least in spirit. But his lips have long since been closed; and it was left to Mr. Handley-Page, the famous manufacturer of more famous aeroplanes, to tell it for him.

It is the story of a British bomber that flew from London to Constantinople; and, after ravaging that mysterious city of domes and minarets, came safely home again.

Officially the affair was mentioned in a Press Bureau message, November 16th, 1917, that:

At Constantinople our machines, in spite of heavy anti-aircraft fire, dropped to a height of 800 feet to attack the *Goeben*. The first salvo of four bombs missed the ship, but hit some submarines and destroyers moored alongside her. The second salvo hit the *Goeben* a little forward of amidships, causing a large explosion and a big conflagration. Our machines then bombed the *General*, in which the German headquarters at Constantinople are reported to be situated. Bombs were dropped from a height of 1,300 feet, and two direct hits were secured on the stern of the ship. The next object of attack was the War Office, on which two direct hits were observed in the centre of the building. The Turkish Minister at Berne has made a statement in reference to these air attacks, in which he acknowledges that the War Office at Constantinople and a destroyer were hit, 'a certain amount of damage being done.'

Mr. Handley-Page gave a somewhat fuller story, at a dinner held in London to celebrate the event. He said that:

Setting out from Hendon, the company of five reached Paris, and flew through France down the Rhone valley to Lyons, and on to Marseilles. From Marseilles they flew to Pisa, and thence to Rome. The battleplane then proceeded to Naples, and on to Otranto. Crossing the Albanian Alps, the aviators flew on to Salonica, and thence to their base to prepare for the final stages of the trip to Constantinople, which involved flying 250 miles over a hostile country under conditions equally arduous as that of Chavez's flight across the Alps.

While flying across the Albanian Alps the airmen could see the hostile Bulgarian horsemen chasing them, in the hope that their machine might be forced to descend and give the crew as prisoners into their hands. Cross winds, clouds, and all kinds of atmospheric disturbances rendered the latter portion of the voyage most difficult and perilous. The mountain peaks range from 8,000 feet to 10,000 feet, in height. Happily, the engines never failed for one moment, and even with the heavy load on board there was never the slightest fear on the part of the pilots that any trouble would arise.

After a short rest at their base, and careful overhauling of the machine, the airmen set out on what was the culminating achievement of their wonderful flight. The bombing of the Turkish capital was done at night. A two-and-a-half hours' journey brought the two pilots and engineer left to man the aeroplane over the Sea of Marmora, and straight up the Sea of Marmora they headed for the attack on the *Goeben* and the Turkish capital itself.

Constantinople was reached when flying at a height of 2,000 feet, and there, lying beneath them, could be seen the Goeben with all lights on and men walking on deck. Constantinople itself was brilliantly *illuminated*. The Golden Horn was clearly silhouetted.

Once the aeroplane flew along a line parallel with the *Goeben*, so as accurately to determine its speed and give the necessary data for bombing. Circling twice, the machine dived down to 800 feet, and a salvo of four bombs was released. The first salvo missed the *Goeben*, but exploded against one or two submarines lying at its side. Again, the aviators flew around, in order to make certain of their aim, and this time they hit the *Goeben* with four bombs.

The dropping of the eight bombs seemed to disconcert the Turks, for all lights suddenly went out. The pilots then made off towards the Golden Horn, and dropped two more bombs on the ship called the *General*, which was the headquarters of the German General Staff. Finally, they flew over the Turkish capital, and dropped two more bombs on the Turkish War Office, which, in the words of the Turkish *communiqué*, 'was not destroyed,'—having been over Constantinople thirty minutes altogether.

Now by this time considerable alarm seems to have been caused in Constantinople, and guns which had not been previously fired were now directed upon the aeroplane. In fact, the flight back to the Sea of Marmora, when Lieutenant McClellan took charge, was accompanied by a fusillade of shrapnel and explosive shells, and on arrival at the base it was found that no fewer than twenty-six bullets had penetrated the machine. One lucky shot partially disabled part of the oiling system of one engine, and the return flight was carried out with the second engine alone.

(*Vide The Goeben & the Breslau*: The Imperial German Navy in the Mediterranean, 1914—The Flight of the Goeben and Breslau: Leonaur 2020.)

Exploits in the Air

by E W Walters

FLIGHT-COMMANDER WILLIAM LEAFE ROBINSON, V.C.

Flight-Commander William Leafe Robinson, V.C, was the first air-man to bring down a German airship on British soil, and he enjoyed the distinction of being the first soldier to win the Victoria Cross in England. The raid during which his heroic act was performed was carried out by thirteen airships in the early part of September, 1916. The principal theatre of operations was the Eastern Counties, and the objectives seem to have been London and certain industrial centres in the Midlands. The new measures taken for the reduction or obscuration of light undoubtedly proved most efficacious, for the raiding squadrons, instead of steering a steady course, as in the raids of the spring and autumn of 1915, groped about in darkness, looking for a safe avenue of approach to their objectives. Three airships only were able to approach the outskirts of London. One of them appeared over the northern district at about 2.15 a.m., where she was at once picked up by searchlights and heavily engaged by anti-aircraft guns and aeroplanes. After a few minutes this airship was seen to burst into flames and to fall rapidly towards the earth.

Not, however, till some hours had elapsed was the name of the hero of the hour made known. Meanwhile official reports were issued, the first simply announcing the raid, and the second stating that one airship had been brought down in flames near London. On Sunday, September 3, an official report stated that after careful inquiries it had been found that casualties and damage caused by the raid were quite disproportionate to the number of airships employed, the casualties being one man and one woman killed, eleven men and two children injured. No casualties occurred in the Metropolitan District, though some houses and outhouses were slightly damaged. Elsewhere the damage was very small, no military damage of any sort being done.

A great number of persons saw the airship fall. One witness relates that he saw it shortly before two o'clock, and for ten minutes, it seemed to him, it was smothered with shrapnel, held the whole time by a concentration of three or four searchlights. He had watched the bombardment on other visits, but in none of them, he says, did the shells burst in such deadly proximity to their objective. The airship, in his own words, might have been giving her own firework display. He saw the airship make off northwards. Already she was a ship in distress.

She yawed and dipped—first this end and then that—going, all the time, at a good speed. Then she was lost behind a cloud. A long silence ensued. The sky was full of cloud patches. The searchlights were all shut off. Suddenly the airship was seen far to the northward. She had travelled behind a sheltering cloud. She slipped from its edge, and the searchlights had her at once. It was seen that she was falling. She must have been from 2,000 to 3,000 feet up. She had fallen a little, when suddenly she burst into flames! The light was everywhere. Had your back been to it, or your eyes shut, you must have been sensible of it. The thing fell like the moon falling from heaven, with a long trail of light—only the light was crimson, not green—and as it fell there broke out one of the most eerie sounds ever heard—hand-clapping and cheering from thousands of people all round, whose waking existence one had never suspected in the dark until that moment. They applauded simultaneously as at a pageant, till the sky over London seemed as full of cheering as it had been full of the rosy strange light only a moment before.

There are many other interesting and instructive accounts. A special constable, who witnessed the raid, writes:

It was at about 11.30 p.m. when I heard the first Zeppelin. I could not, however, see any airship owing to the mist intervening. Several aeroplanes continued to cruise around at great heights with only their little tail lights discernible. People were beginning to return to bed on the assumption that the raid was over, when soon after two o'clock bombs were heard dropping again—this time in the direction of London—together with the noise of heavy anti-aircraft bombardment. We now saw the airship easily just over the north-eastern outskirts of London in the rays of many searchlights.

After some minutes of very heavy gunfire, she made a graceful sweep and turned tail, going full speed eastwards for home and safety. But though she must have been about 8,000 feet up at this time the searchlights followed with relentless persistency, while all the time the guns were barking madly after her. Then a strange thing occurred. The airship suddenly disappeared and reappeared again—caught up apparently by new searchlights further along the line of its retreating course. She looked much smaller than before. At about the same time a strange red light appeared in the sky almost directly above the airship and the guns immediately ceased to fire. The searchlights never left the invader for an instant now. The hundreds of thousands of people who were again out of doors and witnessing this new and weird development held their breath. Everybody seemed to feel that something dramatic was about to occur.

Suddenly a flame flashed out from one end of the airship, and almost at the same time she began a nose dive towards the earth, the flame growing and spreading throughout the whole length of her immense body. It was a wonderful, unforgettable sight. The flames lit up the sky and land for miles and miles around with a brilliant red hue as the million and half or so cubic feet of hydrogen were being devoured by the hungry flames. I could read a newspaper with ease in this light, though I was more than ten miles away. The airship took quite two minutes dropping to earth, but during those two minutes mad, deafening cheers rose out of the night from all sides. Hooters from works and from vessels in the Thames and railways shrieked and whistled and screeched, all joining in the general pandemonium of joy.

Even from a distance of five miles away I could hear the deep-throated cheers of the Irish Guards in camp there. For a full half-hour the cheering continued, echoing and re-echoing from all sides, and in the intervals of the joyous shouts of half-dressed men, women, and children could be heard the humming of an aeroplane's uncommonly powerful engines. Again, the mysterious red light appeared: then a white light and again a red light, and so on alternately, until the multitude realised that the victor of a great air battle was returning, signalling the story of his success as he made for his aerodrome headquarters, guided by friendly searchlights. Then again, such cheers rent the air as may not have ever been heard before anywhere on earth in the blackness of a very early September morning.

A crowd of persons from a radius of almost twenty miles flocked hastily to the scene of the wreckage. One records how:

An engine, salved with the two halves of a propeller from the wreckage, lay by the side of a hedge. Men were measuring them with their walking-sticks and women by the length of their umbrellas. Pieces of wood and aluminium had been shot hel-ter-skelter all over the field and were being gathered up as grim yet precious treasures. A cordon, half military, half constabulary, kept the onlookers at a distance of some twenty yards. And all the time the flames were steadily consuming the framework of the terror of the air.'

How the monster met her end was described by one who saw all that happened:

She was flying at a great height, but the anti-aircraft guns were putting in splendid work. Not once, nor twice, but many times the airship seemed to be hit, until the *gondola* must have been riddled through and through. She reeled. Then she shook herself like some great angry animal enraged at attack, but not disposed to turn and flee. Probably she couldn't fly away, even at that time. Anyway, she made no attempt. The airship burst into flames in the centre first, then at the ends. She sank lower and lower, and at last, tumbling over with nose pointing downward, she fell to the earth with no bump or thud. The dull splash of an incendi-ary bomb and the cracking report of what was left of her am-munition were the only noises she made as her dying gasps.
When the crowd did talk of the awful thing that lay smoulder-ing in the long damp grass they were emphatic in two direc-tions. Men of our own Flying Corps, who know the perils of the air from experience, paid splendid tribute to the memory of the charred dead who lay doubled up in the attitudes of the final agony. "Whatever they meant to do, whatever they had done, they were brave men," said one. From others of the spectators came what was, perhaps, not unnatural—satisfaction undisguised.

People who saw the airship in full flight agreed that she was flying very high—much higher indeed than the airship which previously visited London. From the earth she looked like a small illuminated cigar set thousands of feet above the countryside. Directly she was sighted in the northern districts of London several large searchlights held her while the guns got to work. There was an incessant gunfire for a few minutes, and then there was silence. The airship had fled north. But in the course of the next few moments the lights picked her up again. Then was seen the mysterious signalling light of our heroic airmen.

The village of Cuffley, made famous by the fall of the airship, is a little village of tiled cottages resting in the curve of a white road which defines the crest of a splendid sweeping hill crowned with poplars and tall pines.

The contour of the village is that of a wide, clearly determined triangle, with the church and the inn marking the base and the cottage of Castle Farm placed at the apex.

> The shadow of the little grey church falls athwart the yard of the inn, by name The Plough; but Castle Farm is divided from it by two smooth, rich meadows.

A footpath crosses these meadows, uniting the farm and the inn.

The burning airship fell into a big field which lies in the direct centre of the triangle. This is a barren field; the very soil is black and unfertile, covered with tall grass, grey and parched. The splintered blades of the airship's propeller crashed through a hedge, tearing it and breaking it down. One writes:

> Such was the damage done, such was the fine quality of the mercy meted out to the village of Cuffley.

One of the villagers records:

> I was running downstairs at the time the airship was falling. The whole house was lighted up. I saw all of the furniture in the hall, and the table and the carpet. My husband was down there. He hadn't had time to get dressed. He was putting on his clothes down there in the hall. They were all streaked with red, his face and his hands, too. The red light stopped, but it was still light—just a little light.
> I could hear him talking. I was trying to ask him what he was saying, but my tongue wouldn't move in my mouth. I was shaking all over. I thought I was going to fall down the stairs—the

steps in our house are very crooked.

"We are lost—we are lost!" I said. But my husband says I said nothing at all. I'm sure I don't know.

"We must get out of here," he said, "It'll be on us in a minute." But we couldn't get the front door unlocked. We were trying to break it open, hammering on it. And I was wondering all the time if it was going to fall through the roof. I thought it was hours we were there. "What a dreadful way to die," I said. And he said, "There, there, everything's all right."

Then the red light came back in the sky again—and all of the time we couldn't get the door open. But all at once it came open quite easily.

We were out in the yard. We saw a flaming mass drop into the field by The Plough. We thought the people there were killed. We began to run. We could see the fire burning. But nobody was hurt—what a wonderful thing! I felt almost happy—but I knew I shouldn't be happy when such an awful thing had happened.

My husband took me with him into the field. He said I couldn't stand to see those things out there. But I thought that when it's war everybody can stand everything. And I didn't know—maybe, somebody had been hurt. You couldn't tell, you know—somebody might need help.

Another villager records that the airship just missed The Plough, and fell in a field close by.

When we got over to the field, we could still hear the *crack, crack, crack* of the cartridges exploding in the fire. This must have kept up for about twenty minutes. The thing I was thinking was that there wasn't much of a wreck there for an airship—only about twenty-five square yards of it. I had a great fear at the back of my mind that it might be one of our smaller airships, after all. Then we found the propeller. We saw four bodies burning in the wires—they were all black and charred, still burning. There's no doubt about it—not a man in that airship came down alive. There was a lot of burnt wood sticking in the ground everywhere around—everything had stuck in the ground end on. We even saw a broken Thermos flask.

It is well that these statements of eyewitnesses, which with the passing of time will take on peculiar interest, should be set down in these pages.

In appraising the heroic achievement of Flight-Commander Robinson, V.C., we should bear in mind that night flying presents peculiar difficulties. A contributor to *The Aeroplane,* October 11, 1916, writes:

> The actual bodily peril of flying at night may not be as great as is the peril of crossing the German lines in broad daylight, but the nerve strain must be greater. The aviator over the German side of the lines has generally something on hand to keep him from brooding, such as a battle with a German machine or the dodging of good shooting, and he generally has a passenger by way of company. The night pilot, on the other hand, flies entirely alone. He flaps around for hours on end, with nothing to do but think and keep a look-out for other aircraft. And nothing is so great a strain on the nerves as unlimited time for thinking, a pastime for which the pilot has considerable leisure, now that all respectable aeroplanes are inherently stable.
>
> If there is any mist about, there is the constant danger of collision with other machines, for in the dark there is not even that chance of dodging which a pilot gets from the few seconds during which he can see another aeroplane approaching in a cloud which is illuminated by daylight. Over and above it all is the constant imminence of the landing problem, with the prospect of being smashed up, and possibly burnt to death, if the pilot makes a mistake, or fortune is against him.

Flight-Commander Robinson showed remarkable skill as well as great valour—a hero in the good British sense of the word. On September 3 he had the honour of being foremost at the investiture at Windsor Castle, when the king decorated him with the Victoria Cross.

The first of the money rewards received from grateful admirers of his valour was £500 from Mr. L. A. Oldfield. Mr. William Bow also sent the £500 which he offered to the first pilot to bring down an enemy airship on British soil. A further £2,000 came from Col. Joseph Cowen, and public recognition was made by Sir Charles Cheers Wakefield, Lord Mayor of London. All united in paying a tribute to the young aviator's heroic deed.

We have seen that he bore his honours with fine spirit. He claimed for himself no peculiar gifts of gallantry or skill. It was, he said, merely his good fortune. There were many, he said, waiting for the opportunity to do what he had done. Later the opportunity came, and we know to our just pride that amongst our airmen there are *many* heroes.

Lieutenant Frederick Sowrey, D.S.O., and Lieutenant Alfred Brandon, M.C., D.S.O.

The next raid over England by German airships took place on the night of September 25, 1916. Twelve airships took part, but only ten returned. One was brought down in flames not far from London, the crew being killed; the second came down near the coast, and the crew were made prisoners. Both of the airships were of the latest and largest type.

An official report issued by Lord French stated that probably not more than twelve airships participated in the raid. Police reports from the provinces indicated that the damage done by the raiding airships was slight. At one town in the East Midlands, however, a number of bombs were dropped, and two persons were killed and eleven injured. Some damage was caused at a railway station, and about a dozen houses and shops were wrecked or damaged, and a chapel and a storehouse were set on fire. With this exception no other casualties were reported outside the Metropolitan area, and although a large number of bombs were dropped promiscuously over the districts visited by the airships the material damage was insignificant.

A great number of bombs fell in the sea or in open places. In the Metropolitan area seventeen men, eight women, and three children were killed, forty-five men, thirty-seven women and seventeen children being injured. A considerable number of small dwelling-houses and shops were demolished or damaged, and a number of fires were caused. Two factories sustained injury. Some empty railway trucks were destroyed, and the permanent way was slightly damaged in two places. No reports were received of any *military* damage.

The first definite information that German airships were approaching London was received shortly before eleven o'clock. No sooner was a Zeppelin located than the guns opened fire with apparent accuracy, considering the difficulty of estimating the range. Some of the shells burst very close to the raider, and once it appeared to have been hit. Anyway, after that it lost no time in seeking a higher altitude, where it was lost to sight. Some minutes elapsed before the weird humming of Zeppelin engines was heard again.

Two Zeppelins were now seen making their way in a north-easterly direction. An anti-aircraft gun, which had been following or anticipating their movements, opened fire. The gun was fired as fast as it could be reloaded, and one or two others, at a little distance off, joined in. But owing, perhaps, to their power of emitting dense smoke clouds behind which to escape, the Zeppelins managed to elude their watchers. But once more, after a brief interval, the sounds of the engines could be heard above, and the airships could occasionally be discerned at a great height, as they were revealed by the searchlights making their way back to the coast at what seemed to be the utmost speed of which they were capable. Whether the Zeppelin that was first seen was one of the two which were hit afterwards is not known.

The guns for the defence of London now opened again sharply for a few minutes, and as suddenly relapsed into silence. Faint searchlights flickered here and there, and were withdrawn one or two at a time, when it seemed there was nothing left aloft to search for. But the fleeing Zeppelins were not having it all their own way. Their flight was punctuated by gunfire, which became fainter the farther they went, and they were also pursued by heroic airmen. Then miles away in the distance, and not many degrees above the horizon, the sky began to glow red. 'Then there appeared the nucleus of a brilliant comet falling headlong.' It was visible only for a few seconds, but the spectators raised loud cheers, for they knew that another raiding Zeppelin had met with the fate it deserved so richly, and that another proof had been given to the Germans that Zeppelin raids could not be made with impunity.

Describing the fall in flames of the raider, a Metropolitan special constable writes:

I was on duty on Monday, September 3, when the Zeppelin was brought down at Cuffley, and again during the raid in the early hours of yesterday morning (September 26). I had a particularly clear, though distant, view of both events, which, though they resembled one another in some respects, had at least one important point of difference. When the Cuffley airship took fire, she sailed helpless across the sky, a blazing tomb drifting for miles through the air at an angle which brought her steadily nearer to the ground. That was the first stage. Then her nose dipped, the fire enveloped her completely, and she fell almost perpendicularly; that was the last stage.

But this time the end came more swiftly. I watched one of the Zeppelins under fire for some minutes; in the searchlight beams she looked like an incandescent bar of white-hot steel. Then she staggered, and swung to and fro in the air for just a perceptible moment of time. That, no doubt, was the instant when the damage was done, and the huge craft became unmanageable. Then, without drifting at all from her approximate place in the sky, without any other preliminary, she fell like a stone—first horizontally, then in a position which rapidly became almost perpendicular she went down, a mass of flame. . . . From the place where I was, I could see and hear some of the rejoicings which greeted the victorious end of this latest battle in the air. Policemen, special constables, firemen, and ambulance men had their eyes turned on the combat in the eastern sky, and cheered and cheered again. From houses of all sorts men, women and children ran out in their night-clothes to listen to the bombardment, and to stare at the vast glow which for a few seconds lit up darker London.'

Another special constable writes:

The sky was so clear that the action was apparently fought without the aid of searchlights. The gunfire was continuous, deep and heavy. It in fact became so continuous that sense of excitement faded away, and the people in the streets chatted about home affairs without very much heed of what was going on to the east. But air engagements have the quality of speed. Suddenly we were in the great first act. A cry, a shout, a rush, and all eyes were fixed on the eastern sky. An airship was seen for one moment "riding at anchor," as it were, on level keel, and then it glowed and slowly turned and came quietly down the eastern side a cigar-shaped, red, incandescent mass. The fall seemed much slower than that of September 3, but the distance was much greater, and refraction of the horizon distorted the image. The fall seemed appallingly slow, and towards the end, as it reached the skyline, the ruined airship hung and glowed for many seconds. Then the great shout broke out, the cheering ran across London and must have been heard on the outer hills and down the expectant Thames.

Then followed the eager rush of thousands of persons toward the scene.

A correspondent of the *Times* has told how the wreckage lay athwart a hedge with its lattice framework impaled on an oaktree, looking like the skeleton of some huge primaeval monster:

She had not fallen like the ship which fell at Cuffley Wood. That one crumpled and telescoped until it occupied a space little more than 30 yards square. This lay with her nose crumpled and bent out of shape, but the framework of girders and lattice was strong enough to hold together. All this twisted mass of metal fell its length on the ground. As she lay it did not seem that the fabric was burnt off the gaunt ribs until one noticed pieces of molten aluminium and brass in the debris.

One realised the cost of such a craft looking even at the wreck. Lying on the ground was a red leather cushion. This covered the seat of the engineman, and the ghastly evidences still to be seen showed that he died at his post. One at least of the petrol tanks had burst in half, and the heat of the burning spirit had melted the broken edges until they looked like some fine fretted lace. The airship was built of aluminium girders, and some of the parts were almost massive, although, of course, comparatively light. There were the remains of an air mattress and a blanket, perhaps the bed for one of the night shift when off duty.

Curious evidences of the crew's breakfast still remained. There were slices of bacon and hunks of brown greasy *Kriegsbrod* with delicately sliced potatoes. Even with the subsequent unanticipated cooking the breakfast was not done, so presumably the crew intended to have their meal when they got clear of the coast.

One body was found far out in the field. This was the body of the commander, for although his uniform was burned a little it was still recognisable, and the badges were plain to see. He must have thrown himself over before the ship took her headlong plunge. The other bodies were all dressed in warm clothing, with thick felt boots. Several of the bodies would have been easily recognisable to anyone that had known the men in life, but for the most part they were badly burned. A working party of troops was put on to clear away the wreckage, and it was thought that there were other bodies still under the piled-up debris.

The second raider came down in Essex. Her propeller had been hit, presumably by gunfire, and with the ship unmanageable and the danger of drifting out to sea, the commander was compelled to make a hasty descent.

The special constable who was the first on the scene has given the following account:

> I was on duty near where the Zeppelin fell. I had seen something about 300 yards away, and I was looking about expecting some adventure, when a batch of Germans appeared in the roadway.
>
> I turned my torchlight upon the leading man—the commander—who at once said:
>
> "Can you please tell us the way to—?"
>
> I said, "Oh, yes; just come with me." I walked with the commander, the rest of the crew following, till I saw several other special constables on duty.
>
> The Germans jabbered mostly in their own language as we walked along, but several could speak quite good English.
>
> I asked them how they had managed to land safely.
>
> "Were you hit?" I asked. One grudgingly said something like "*Yah.*" The commander was less talkative about this, though.
>
> By this time, we were approaching my colleagues of the Special Constabulary, and I told them what had happened.
>
> Meanwhile I, of course, told the commander what was really unnecessary under the circumstances—that he was my prisoner. He asked to be brought over to the military. Accompanied by the specials, the crew were handed over to the military.
>
> They were taken in Red Cross motorcars to the detention barracks.

A labourer near whose cottage the Zeppelin fell, when interviewed by the *Daily Mirror*, said that at about half-past one he was roused by the loud drone of a Zeppelin engine—a noise to which residents of this part of the North-east coast have now become accustomed.

He got out of bed and saw the huge bulk of an airship close overhead.

The vessel passed away, but then turned and soon descended in a field near the back of his cottage. The crew got out; and then followed an explosion. The man said:

> It didn't hurt any of us, but it smashed the front windows of my house and those of my neighbours.
>
> I found afterwards that all the hair was singed off the back of my dog, which was in a kennel outside.
>
> Then all the crew came to my cottage and started knocking at the door. I never answered, and I heard the commander shout-

ing. He spoke English, and said something about the house.'

Asked if the German said '*Kamerad*,' the labourer replied, 'I don't know what else he said, but I put my wife and three children in a back room and made myself scarce, too.'

The end of the airship dropped across the road which is by the cottage.

When the Zeppelin came down it was to all appearances intact, though suffering fatally from engine trouble. It had a big bulge upwards and downwards at the middle. Its full shape, however, was still well outlined, though twisted in places. Its engines had dug well into the earth, and a long, thin line indicated it had trailed along the ground for some hundreds of yards before coming to rest outside the cottage.

It is now known that our heroic airmen dealt the death-blows to the raiders. An inhabitant of a South London suburb relates that when our searchlights had spotted the enemy, it was realised by the diminutive appearance of the airship that it was far higher than any yet seen over the outskirts of London. It was travelling quickly, for a time due north, then north-east. Our airmen, hot in pursuit, were seen to be making splendid progress. Not till the 5th of October were the names of the heroic airmen made public. On the day named the following official announcement was made:—

The king has been graciously pleased to appoint the under-mentioned officers Companions of the Distinguished Service Order in recognition of their gallantry and distinguished service in connexion with the successful attack on enemy airships: Sec.-Lieut. Frederick Sowrey, Royal Fusiliers, attached R.F.C. Sec.-Lieut. Alfred De Bath Brandon, M.C., R.F.C. Special Reserve.'

The valour and skill of the aviators was acclaimed on all sides. Lieut. Sowrey, it may be said, is one of three flying brothers, sons of Mr. John Sowrey, Deputy Chief Inspector of Inland Revenue, of Yeoveney Lodge, Staines. Born at Gloucester, he was educated at home until he was thirteen, when he won an open scholarship at King's College School, Wimbledon. Gaining two leaving scholarships, tenable at a university, he went to King's College, where he took the intermediate B.Sc. Degree. He was finishing his graduate course when the war broke out.

He at once volunteered for service, and, joining the infantry, went out early to the Western front. Wounded at Loos, he was invalided home, remaining in hospital about three months. On leaving hospital he joined the Flying Corps, for 'anything with a motor connected with it had always had a great attraction for him.' He had Lieut. Robinson, V.C., as his fellow-learner. He was taking a course for the Indian Civil Service when the war called him into the fighting service.

Lieutenant Brandon is the young New Zealander who in April of the year 1915 assisted in bringing down the Zeppelin L15 in the Thames Estuary. An advertisement of the Hall Flying School at Hendon brought him to England. He answered the advertisement, and was immediately accepted as a pupil. He gained his aeroplane ticket seven weeks after joining the school. Previous to the war he was at Trinity College, Cambridge.

The battle fought by the airmen wag of a thrilling nature. It is recorded that a 'ding-dong' fight ensued, in which Lieut. Sowrey and Lieut. Brandon manoeuvred for position. Lieut. Sowrey had the best of luck, and quickly seized his opportunity of emulating the feat of Lieut. Robinson. Making splendid use of his machine gun, he sent a few well-directed shots into the Zeppelin. Instantly the airship began to turn and twist, and finally crashed to earth a blazing mass. Meanwhile Lieut. Brandon stood by in case of emergency, and later attacked a second raider, which was compelled to surrender.

THE CAPTIVE ZEPPELIN

The Zeppelin which came down in the manner described in the foregoing chapter was on view to a party of London Press Representatives on October 8, 1916. The *Times* representative recalled the fact that the airship lost one of her starboard propellers some while before falling. Although parts of the structure of the airship were crumpled up, the main outlines could be easily recognised. The framework or skeleton was composed of a series of longitudinal lattice-work girders running from end to end and connected at intervals by circular lattice-work ties, the whole structure being bound together and stiffened by means of a system of wires provided with arrangements which enabled them to be tightened up. The material used was an alloy of aluminium.

At the largest point the framework had a diameter of 72 feet, and was of stream-like form, the bow being sensibly blunter than the stern, which, indeed, tapered off to a sharp point. The length of the vessel appeared to have been 650 feet or 680 feet, and the weight complete, with engines, fuel, guns, and ammunition, was calculated at 50 tons. The hydrogen capacity was 2,000,000 cubic feet, and there were 24 ballonets extending the whole length of the ship. Of the envelope only one or two fragments were to be seen, the rest having been burnt. The airship, which was numbered L33, was of quite recent construction, having been built last July, and its cost is estimated by the Admiralty authorities at about a quarter of a million.

How long was required for building it could not be told from an inspection of the remains, but the enormous amount of detail was evident enough. To enable the crew, which consisted of twenty-two men, to move from one part of the ship to another, a cat-walk ran along the keel, enclosed in an arched passage. It consisted of a narrow footway, nine inches in width and made of wood—one of the very few examples of wood construction used—and provision for ventilation was made in the shape of shafts rising to the top of the ship.

In all there were four *gondolas*—one forward, two amidships, and one aft. The first of these constituted the navigating bridge. It was divided into three parts. The first was set apart for the commander, and in it were concentrated the controls of the horizontal and vertical rudders at the stern, the engine-room telegraphs, and the switches for the electrical release of the bombs. These last, of which sixty were carried, were actually arranged amidships, and the sliding door which was opened to allow them to fall could still be seen moving freely on its bearings.

Behind the commander's room in the forward *gondola* was a cabin for the wireless operator, measuring perhaps 6 feet by 4 feet, and behind that again an engine-room containing a 240 h.p. Maybach Mércedès engine having six vertical cylinders. Behind the engine was a clutch, a brake, and a reducing gear, through which the power was transmitted to a propeller shaft; a generator for the wireless installation was placed in front. One similar engine was carried in each of the *gondolas* amidships, and three in the aft *gondola*, all the engines having wireless generators attached. There were thus six engines, with an aggregate power of 1,440 h.p., and six propellers. Of the latter, three were worked from the aft *gondola*, one being placed in the centre at a point distant from the tail about one-fifth of the length of the ship, and the other two one on each side; two were driven from the side *gondolas* amidships, and the sixth was in connexion with the forward *gondola*.

To reduce air-resistance a stream-line form was given to the propeller stays by the aid of a thin two or three-ply wooden casing. The amount of petrol carried was 2,000 gallons, and the speed is supposed to have been about sixty miles an hour in a still atmosphere. The armament, apart from the bombs, consisted of nine quick-firing guns. Of these, two larger than the others were mounted on the roof, two were in the forward *gondola*, one each in the amidships *gondolas*, two in the aft *gondola*, and one in the tail. The lightness of the construction was shown by the fact that the huge tail still containing the remains of the gun platform could easily be rolled over.

In addition to the particulars given there were other interesting features. It may be noted, for instance, that practically everything, except the engines and the guns, was made of aluminium alloy. The only woodwork was the narrow platform, known as the 'cat-walk,' which ran along the keel and connected the *gondolas*. It was closed in with fibre. There was a little wood also in the ventilators, which were found intact. The wood was covered with Manchester cotton, which looked like common sheeting, but was really of very fine texture. The pressure of a button in the captain's cabin opened the sliding grille of framework, and an electrical device permitted each bomb to be dropped separately, either slowly or rapidly.

Lieutenant W. K. Tempest, D.S.O.

Concerning the raid over England by hostile airships which took place on the night of October 2, 1916, the official report issued by Lord French was to the effect that ten hostile airships crossed the East Coast between nine p.m. and midnight. One airship approached the north of London about ten p.m., but was driven off by gunfire and pursued by aeroplanes. She attempted to return from the northwest, but was attacked by guns and aeroplanes and brought to earth in flames in the neighbourhood of Potter's Bar shortly before midnight.

An eye-witness of the fall of the airship writes, (*Times*, Oct. 3, 1916):

> I live in the country just outside the fringe of the great searchlights which guard the London area. From the verandah of the house one can obtain a wonderful view of any "pyrotechnic" display within a distance of twenty odd miles. The household is most familiar with Zeppelins, aeroplanes, bombs, guns, and searchlights. We have seen all the raids, we have seen three Zeppelins destroyed, and bombs have fallen all round us; but happily, our little district has so far escaped damage. So accustomed are we to all these aerial affairs that we seem to know instinctively when a raid is due. And it was so on Sunday. The sky at eight o'clock looked very ominous.

Sometime later came the warning to the special constables, and at the same time the sky in our immediate neighbourhood was lit up by powerful rays from searchlights. I rightly surmised that the Zeppelin would attempt to reach London from the north. By now (I live close to the railway) the searchlights were sweeping the cloudless sky, and the air was quite still. About half-past ten we heard the beat of the Zeppelin engines; she was due north of the house. Then she sailed towards the east. The night was so clear that she was seen quite easily. With the aid of a night glass, she appeared about a yard long.

By the sound of her engines we could tell she was circling the fringe of light, for she gradually altered her course from east to south-east. Then we heard her wheel round to the left. She made a circle of some miles, and finally went south-east again, when we heard the engines no more. Meanwhile my children, two girls, aged eight and eleven, insisted on dressing: they wanted to "see the show." With their mother they made themselves comfortable on the verandah. About half-past eleven, away to the south-east, we saw flashes from falling bombs, and the bursting of shrapnel, with the boom of heavy guns firing. The children were getting very interested.

Suddenly a score of searchlights seemed to concentrate at one point, and quite distinctly we saw the Zeppelin "held." Shrapnel was bursting all around her. Then the guns ceased, and we could see no Zeppelin. We thought she had managed to slip away. But our airmen were on her track, and soon there appeared a yellow light; it became larger and larger, until we realised that it was the Zeppelin alight. From yellow the flames changed to ruby; they seemed to spread from the centre to each end of the airship. When she was aglow from end to end, she tilted, gradually became perpendicular, and fell slowly to earth. The flames lit, up the country for miles; the framework of the machine was plainly visible. You could see smaller portions of her ribs, loosened by the heat, falling like small sparks. She fell five miles from my house, but I thought I heard the whole of England cheering.

Another witness, who watched the coming of the raider from the north-east, has given the following account:

What struck me was the evident uncertainty of the crew as to where they were, or where they wanted to go. They stopped; they turned this way and that; they manoeuvred in every direction in order to avoid the searchlights which were darting about all round them. But it was all to no purpose. The way in which the great beams of light followed the airship in all its desperate efforts to escape was really wonderful. A few moments passed, and the guns began to shell the Zeppelin. The shells burst all round—some of them so near that it seemed as though hits had been scored. Then, in a moment, a bright light burst out in the body of the airship, and in another moment, she was a mass of flame from end to end. She seemed to turn over on her side, and then gradually sink to earth.

While coming down, she broke into halves, and during the descent she threw off huge bunches of some flaming material. From the great height at which she had been floating it was impossible to tell where she would come down, and for some moments the onlookers did not know but that she might fall upon them. But the blazing remains plunged at length behind some trees, and that is the last we saw of her.

The nearest view of this fourth airship debacle on British soil was enjoyed by a farmer at Potters Bar, on whose farm the Zeppelin came down. He has given the following interesting account:

We were awakened by the sound of the guns, and we got up. I went into my garden, and from where I stood the Zeppelin seemed to be right overhead. Thinking that she might be preparing to drop bombs, I brought my wife and two children into the garden away from the house. We had not been watching it many moments before the airship suddenly burst into flame. It was then apparently right over my house, and looked as though it would fall right across the roof. It was burning furiously, and, blazing masses were flying away from it during its descent. I shouted to my wife to be prepared to run out into the road in case it should fall upon the house. But as it got lower and lower—it did not seem to fall very quickly—I saw it would fall into the fields behind my farm buildings.

I ran through the stable yard and down a by lane leading to some grass fields. In the corner of one of these were some large haystacks, and I was afraid that these might be set on fire. When I reached the spot, I found they were all right; but about 200 yards away the remains of the Zeppelin lay blazing furiously. I dared not go very near to it for two reasons: one was that the heat was very great, and another was that ammunition of some kind was exploding at intervals. I afterwards discovered that this was machine-gun ammunition, a large quantity of which seems to have been carried, for some was found in boxes unexploded. I only saw one bomb drop before the Zeppelin came down, but others were found among the debris.

The Zeppelin had broken into two pieces. The larger half was hanging over a big oak tree, which stood in the middle of the field. I saw some dead bodies lying about. One appeared to be that of an officer, for I could see gold stripes on the arm of his coat. Another was wearing the Iron Cross. Some of them had wrapped themselves up in blankets, evidently trying to avoid the flames. I had a herd of valuable dairy cows in the field, and these were very much alarmed at the blazing Zeppelin. They galloped round the field in terror, and one of them seemed determined to rush into the burning mass. I had some difficulty in keeping her away, and I was very glad when the fire brigade came on the scene and began to throw water on the ruins.

There were many interesting incidents connected with the fall of this airship. An Iron Cross was picked up close by. The commander of the airship was wearing a wrist watch which had stopped at 1.20 (German time). One member of the crew, whose body was recovered, appeared to be a boy of sixteen or seventeen years of age. The heat of the wreckage was so great that full search was impossible till over twelve hours had elapsed after the fall. No less than thirty-nine bombs were dropped over one small area to the north of London. Most of the bombs fell, however, in fields and meadows.

The airship was thwarted in its evil designs by our heroic airmen. In the course of a few days, it was officially announced that Second-Lieutenant Wulstan Joseph Tempest, General List and Royal Flying Corps, had been appointed a Companion of the D.S.O., in recognition of conspicuous gallantry and devotion to duty in connexion with the destruction of an enemy airship.

On the fateful day Lieutenant Tempest had finished his regular duties, and was spending the evening with friends at a dinner party. Before the meal was over a call reached him, and a few minutes later he was back at his aerodrome.

He made a speedy start, with the idea of intercepting the airship, which was reported to be approaching. He had soon reached a height of upwards of 10,000 feet. He manoeuvred around unwearying in a protracted vigil.

At the end of two hours a searchlight picked out the airship and persistently stuck to it, despite its efforts to get beyond the focus of the beam. Soon other searchlights added to the volume of illumination, and anti-aircraft guns began to pepper at the airship.

In a moment a great sheet of fire swept along the airship, and it began to fall at a speed increasing as the law of gravitation came into play. Immediately after the Zeppelin caught fire Lieut. Tempest travelled the complete length of the airship from stem to stern, being parallel with it all the time.

Then he began to descend. But the falling airship hampered his movements very considerably. Once or twice he narrowly escaped collision with the flaming mass, and in order to avoid this he was compelled to resort to nose-diving.

The work had been done under tremendous strain, but Lieut. Tempest fortunately escaped injury of any kind. The spot where he landed was miles away from the place where he had first taken the air. Without troubling to examine the burning airship, which had fallen not far away, Lieut. Tempest was driven back to his home station in a side-car, arriving about 2.30 a.m. Here he received a tremendous welcome from his brother-officers as the third man of the same flight who had brought down a Zeppelin.

Lieutenant Tempest was born on January 22, 1890. He was educated at Stonyhurst, and afterwards entered the Mercantile Marine and received training on the *Worcester*. He learned to fly at one of the military schools, taking his pilot's certificate on May 22 of the year of his heroic deed. He had previously been attached to the King's Own Yorkshire Light Infantry, and was invalided home after fighting in France last year at Ypres. For nearly twenty-four hours he was buried in a dug-out, and as a consequence he is still liable to attacks from rheumatic gout. The experience also left him a little lame, but he still retains great skill and courage, and certainly takes high rank amongst our heroic aviators.

LIEUTENANT WARNEFORD, V.C.

To Lieutenant Warneford, V.C, falls the distinction of being one of the first airmen to destroy a Zeppelin. At the time of his heroic deed, he was on patrol duty in Belgium, and, it seems, was under orders to await the return of raiding airships from England. After a long and trying vigil he sighted a Zeppelin, and made straight for a position above the giant structure.

The attack, we must remember, was made in the year previous to the successful exploits dealt with in other chapters. At the time certain improvements in guns and cartridges had not come into use. Lieutenant Warneford's only hope of completely destroying the airship was to drop a bomb on it from above, and this he did with remarkable skill and courage.

On gaining the desired position, he dropped a bomb with such effect that an explosion immediately followed. His bravery will be fully appreciated when we recall the fact that so violent was the explosion that his machine was turned completely over, compelling him to 'loop-the-loop.' This he did with coolness and skill, and although under great difficulties he succeeded in bringing about a safe landing. Unfortunately, he was compelled, owing to engine trouble, to land on territory occupied by the Germans. Good fortune, however, favoured him. He managed, before the appearance on the scene of enemy troops, to restart the motor and again take to the air. It is generally thought that he was assisted by Belgians, but this does not appear to be established. It is, in any circumstances, sufficient to know that the heroic young aviator managed to escape and return safely to his base, there to receive the enthusiastic congratulations of his comrades.

The stricken airship unfortunately fell upon a monastery, doing much damage and killing a number of the inmates. It was a Zeppelin of notable type, carrying an exceptionally large crew, including some of Germany's most efficient engineers.

The news of the destruction of the airship was communicated almost immediately to England, causing keen interest and delight. Lieutenant Warneford became the hero of the hour. The King telegraphed the honour of the Victoria Cross, and the heroic young pilot thus came into the distinction of being the first airman to win the coveted decoration. England and France united in honouring him, and hopes were widely expressed that fresh deeds of valour would be performed in coming days.

But Lieutenant Warneford tasted earthly fame for only a few brief hours. Shortly after his heroic deed, whilst flying with an American journalist as passenger, his machine suddenly swerved, and in some way never fully explained, control was lost, and the machine dashed to

LIEUTENANT WARNEFORD, V.C.

FLIGHT-COMMANDER WILLIAM LEAFE ROBINSON, V.C

earth, killing both the pilot and passenger.

Deep regret was expressed by every friend of the Allies. Much hope had been centred in the courageous young pilot, and the end had come with terrible suddenness. People could not understand. But above all there shone brightly, and still shines, the deed of that *one glorious hour,* when self was forgotten and only duty called.

The name and fame of Lieutenant Warneford will surely live in the annals of aviation—a fearless spirit, quick and strong to act, tasting for a brief while of conquest and fame, and then meeting, all unexpected, a sudden and untimely end. 'Fame,' it is written, 'may fade, but not the great deeds that bring true fame; their influence lasts through all time.' Lieutenant Warneford' s heroic act is not dead. His example has inspired and will continue to inspire, and to him we owe in no small measure many of the more recent deeds of our heroic airmen.

Flight-Commander Albert Ball, D.S.O., M.C.

Few airmen have a finer record than the young British officer, Flight-Commander Albert Ball, who for a while held a commission in the Notts and Derby Regiment, and later was attached to the Royal Flying Corps with the rank of Flight-Commander. He is a native of Nottingham, and joined the Sherwood Foresters as a private at the outbreak of the war. He has brought down no fewer than twenty-nine German aeroplanes and a Drachen observation balloon.

He is only twenty years of age at the time of writing (October, 1916), and is probably one of the smallest flying officers in the service—a small man with great courage. He has black hair, the eyes of a hawk, and a jaw that spells two words—determination and fearlessness.

During a brief period of leave in England he had with him two noteworthy mascots—the propeller of the aeroplane in which he brought down fourteen hostile machines, and a mascot in the form of a large red nose-cap of steel. The Germans know this mascot well.

Whilst on his visit to England he said that his most 'sporting fight' was one in which he and his opponent went at each other for over half an hour. Then, when the ammunition had all gone, the two flew side by side and grinned at one another in mutual admiration. Lieut. Ball said:

We flew together in that way for quite a long distance, exchanging air greetings.

Good fortune has, of course, played a part in Lieut. Ball's many successes. He has himself been forced down several times, but thus far not once has he suffered any personal injury.

His exploits have won him the D.S.O., the Military Cross, the bar to the D.S.O., and the Russian St. George's Cross, which is our Allies' equivalent to the English Victoria Cross. The D.S.O. was bestowed on him for attacking seven enemy machines which he saw flying in formation. One of them he shot down at fifteen yards range, and the others retired.

Immediately afterwards, seeing five more hostile machines, he attacked one at about ten yards range and shot it down. He then attacked another of the machines which had been firing at him, and shot it down into a village. Still not satisfied, he flew to the nearest aerodrome for more ammunition, and returning attacked three more machines.

The bar to the D.S.O. was awarded for subsequent acts of gallantry. On one occasion, observing twelve enemy machines in formation, Commander Ball dived in among them and fired a drum into the nearest machine, which went down out of control. Several more hostile machines then approached, and he fired three more drums at them, driving down another.

The record of this heroic young aviator is indeed remarkable, and one is not surprised when one learns that the British Commander-in-Chief, Sir Douglas Haig, has written to the young hero as follows:

"Well done! D. H."!

LIEUTENANT ALLAN BOTT, M.C.

Lieutenant Allan Bott, who has been awarded the Military Cross for gallantry and devotion to duty in the field, is a member of the editorial staff of the *Daily Chronicle*, and when war broke out acted for a time as a special correspondent in France and Switzerland. He went to Lake Constance to investigate the building of super-Zeppelins, and while at Kreuzlingen, a small Swiss town which is really a suburb of Constance, made an involuntary trip into Germany by entering the wrong train. He spent some hours in Constance, and managed to escape detection at the frontier by travelling under the seat of a cab driven by a friendly Swiss who was going back to Kreuzlingen.

On his return to England, in November, 1914, Mr. Bott joined the O.T.C., and after training received a commission in the R.G.A., whence he transferred to the Royal Flying Corps, Since the deeds which have won Mr. Bott the Military Cross he has been promoted from the rank of Second-Lieutenant to Lieutenant. The story of his

BOMB DROPPING.

The dropping of aerial bombs is a more or less haphazard affair, and unless the target is a big one, such as a town or dock-yard, it is exceedingly difficult to take aim with any degree of accuracy.

flight on a blazing aeroplane has been told modestly by the young officer in a letter to his parents:

All at once our fuselage shivered, and looking down it, I saw that Archie had left his card in the form of a piece of burning H.E.

"Fuselage burning—pass the fire extinguisher," I shouted down the speaking-tube to my pilot. But the pilot's earpiece had slipped from his cap during the dive, and he heard nothing. I stood up, leaned across and shook his shoulder. "Pass the fire extinguisher," I yelled.

"Hun down on the left," he shouted back, my words having been lost in the roar of the engine.

"Fire extinguisher," I called again.

"Why don't you fire at that Hun?" was the reply.

Seeing that the flames were licking their way back to the tail, I abandoned the attempt to get the extinguisher, and crawled down the fuselage to the scene of the fire. I managed to beat out the flames, which had eaten half-way through one of the longerons.

Meanwhile, the pilot had been attacking one of the enemy machines, and a bullet had gone into our petrol tank. Confronted with a diminishing pressure, we decided to make for Allied territory at once, and turned west.

Five minutes later, by which time the number of revolutions had dropped alarmingly, we found the way barred by two more Boche machines. My gun having jammed, the pilot did the only thing possible—he went straight at the nearest German, firing all the time. The Boche swerved just in time to avoid a collision, but had obviously been hit, for his machine all but did a nose-dive, and he only landed with great difficulty.

Then our engine petered out altogether, and there was nothing for it but to do a long glide and try to reach the lines. We were at 4,000 feet when we started to glide, and for a long time we didn't know if we had sufficient height to get us across.

But the pilot took advantage of a small salient, and we managed to glide over the trenches at a height of about 400 yards, fired at by machine-guns and rifles, besides dear old Archie. We landed just behind the second-line trenches of a certain part of the French line, and, to our joy and astonishment, we were not shelled on the ground.

It was an exciting adventure, showing the mettle of our aviators. There have been many such thrilling incidents on the various battle-fronts, some coming to light and winning well-deserved awards, others going to make up the great and glorious number of unrecorded deeds of gallantry.

FLIGHT-LIEUTENANT GUYNEMER

We learn from the *Matin* that the French champion, Flight-Lieutenant Guynemer, once brought down three German aeroplanes in the record time of three minutes, and then himself had an extremely narrow escape from death. He was 3,000 yards up when a shell burst full in one of the wings of his aeroplane, and the frail bird seemed mortally wounded. The whole left wing was completely cut to bits, and the canvas fluttered in the wind, making the rent still worse. In a few seconds there was nothing left on the frame but a piece of canvas the size of a pocket-handkerchief.

The machine fell with a crash through space—it would not support its pilot any longer. Lieutenant Guynemer declares that he gave himself up for lost; the only thing he asked Providence for was that he should not fall in enemy territory. He has said:

I was powerless to make my will felt. My machine refused to obey me. At 1,600 yards I determined to make a fight for it all the same.

The wind had brought me back into our own lines. I was almost happy. I had been thinking of my funeral, with sorrowing friends walking behind my last remains. I had nothing more to fear from the "*pickelhauben.*" However, I felt that it was death, and that thought is not a very pleasant one.

My fall continued. In spite of all my efforts, I could not do what I wanted with my machine. I tried to turn it first to the right and then to the left. I pushed and pulled, but all to no purpose. I could do nothing.

Down I fell, faster and faster, drawn surely and inevitably to the earth, where I was going to be smashed to atoms.

I shut my eyes, then I opened them again and looked down. At something like 110 miles an hour I crashed into a pylon. There was a terrific cracking sound and a deep thud. I looked round and found that nothing was left of my machine.

How is it I am still alive? I wonder myself. I think it was the straps which held me in my seat which saved my life. They had eaten right into my shoulders anyhow, but if it had not been for them, I should be dead at this moment.

Only to the fortunate is it given to relate their experiences. Sudden and untimely death overtakes many heroic pilots, sealing their lips and robbing the world of personal records of their deeds. We are indeed fortunate in having from Flight-Lieutenant Guynemer a story so thrilling. He is one of our gallant Allies' most courageous and skilful pilots, and in aviation France is second to none. Later, we shall afresh see how rich she is in skilful and heroic airmen, and we shall see in particular how well the heroic aviator, Lieutenant Guynemer, has continued to acquit himself.

Lieutenant Stewart Gordon Ridley

It has been said that the story of Second-Lieutenant Ridley, a young British flying officer, is as great as the story of Captain Gates.

Captain Oates walked into the Antarctic blizzard so that his comrades should have a better chance of living. Lieutenant Ridley, stranded in the burning Libyan Desert with an air mechanic, and seeing his tiny stock of water near its end, shot himself in the hope that his companion might live.

The heroic young aviator went out singly on a machine from an oasis in the Libyan Desert as an escort to another pilot, who was accompanied by Air-Mechanic J. A. Garside. After flying for an hour and a half, the party failed to locate the camel patrol which had been sent out in advance to establish a temporary landing-place.

They encamped for the night. The next morning it was found that Lieutenant Ridley's engine would not work, and it was agreed that the other pilot should try to discover the track of the camel patrol. He left his water and provisions with the others, and arranged to return on the following day. The pilot picked up the camel patrol, but when he returned to find Lieutenant Ridley and Garside they had disappeared.

Search parties, consisting of camel patrols, motor-cars, and aeroplanes were at once sent out. Nothing was discovered of the missing men until four days after the start of the original mission, when, twenty-five miles away from the spot where the first night had been spent, a second landing-place was found. The two men had evidently flown away again after patching up their machine. Two days later a motor party found the machine and the two dead bodies of the aviators.

During the search the footprints of the two men had been discovered. They were noticed to have been overtaken by a hostile camel patrol, and for a time it was believed that Lieutenant Ridley and Garside had been captured.

A diary kept by Garside throws peculiar light on the moving story:—

★★★★★★★★★★★★★★★★

Friday.—Mr. Gardiner left for Meheriq, and said he would come and pick one of us up. After he went, we tried to get the machine going, and succeeded in flying for about twenty-five minutes. Engine then gave out. We tinkered engine up again, succeeded in flying about five miles next day, but engine ran short of petrol.

Sunday.—After trying to get engine started, but could not manage it owing to weakness, water running short—only half a bottle—Mr. Ridley suggested walking up to the hills.

Six p.m.—Found it was further than we thought; got there eventually: very done up. No luck. Walked back; hardly any water, about a spoonful. Mr. Ridley shot himself at 10.30 on Sunday while my back was turned. No water all day; don't know how to go on; dozed all day, feeling very weak; wish someone would come; cannot last much longer.

Monday.—Thought of water in compass, got half bottle; seems to be some kind of spirit. Can last another day. Fired Lewis gun, about four rounds; shall fire my "Very light" today: last hope without machine comes. Could last days if had water.

★★★★★★★★★★★★★★★★

On the following day the bodies were discovered by a motorcar.

The Commander of the Imperial Camel Corps reports that from what he discovered he has formed the opinion that Lieutenant Ridley gave his life in the hope of saving the mechanic. Added to this, the commanding officer of the Royal Flying Corps states:

There is no doubt in my mind that he did this in an act of self-sacrifice in the hope of saving the other man.

Lieutenant Ridley, who was affectionately known as 'Riddles' in the corps, came of a celebrated Northumbrian family, one of his ancestors being Bishop Ridley, who, bound to the stake at Oxford, 'played the man' with Latimer amid the flames. A sympathetic admirer of this gallant officer states:

It may well be, that there came across the desert from Gordon at Khartoum a message in the words of Latimer, "Be of good cheer, Master Gordon, and play the man."

The fallen hero was a young man of attractive appearance and great charm of manner. His character, as known to intimate friends, confirms in all respects the interpretation put upon his last act, 'He gave his life in the hope that his companion might be saved.'

Both Lieutenant S. G. Ridley and Air-Mechanic J. A. Garside were unmarried, but Garside was the only son of a widowed mother, and evidently in the mind of his heroic companion had special claims upon life.

A chaplain with a party of service men paid the last honours. At the head of the grave a cross was erected.

Sous-Lieutenant Louis Noël

An Army Order, signed by General Sarrail, describes how Lieutenant Noël, when hardly convalescent from a grave operation, from the effects of which he was still suffering, effected on two occasions the bombardment of an enemy capital, and assured a long-distance link between two friendly armies, covering 1,100 kilometres (roughly 700 miles) there and back, of which 850 kilometres (over 500 miles) were over enemy territory.

Lieutenant Noël is an old pilot, remarkable for his address, his bravery, his coolness, and his modesty. Numerous difficult and perilous missions in France and in the Orient have been successfully carried out by him, and in addition to the Cross of the Legion of Honour he has earned the *Médaille Militaire*, the *Croix de Guerre*, and the Russian Cross of St. George.

Describing his remarkable flight from Salonica to Bukarest, a Roumanian journal (September 16, 1916) says:

Roumania received yesterday the visit of gracious Allied winged guests, who come to us from Salonique, from the heroic army of Sarrail, from that corner of ground which, right in the heart of the Balkans, sinks in like a vice, to choke in its powerful grip the Bulgars and our common enemies. As legitimate reprisal for the cowardly attack on Bukarest by the Zeppelins, the French aviators had received orders to bombard Sofia and reach Roumania afterwards. Yesterday, Wednesday, at 6.20 a.m., four French *avions* left Salonique. The first, a Farman biplane, was conducted by the heroic Sous-Lieutenant Noël, one of the best aviators of the French Army, who had already sunk two German *avions* in the course of seventeen months passed on the German front. The Sous-Lieutenant Noël brought with him Lieutenant Leseur, one of the best observers of the Army of Salonique. The second biplane was mounted by Sergeant Lamprou and the Soldier-Machine-Gunner Masson; the third by the Lieutenant Quillery and an observer, and the fourth by the Sergeant Rohan and a machine-gunner.

At 8.40 the Noël biplane arrived above Sofia, where were to be seen several fires lighted by one of the French *avions* which had just passed. The Lieutenant Leseur let go many bombs. The aviators were perfectly guided by the sparkling dome of the cathedral. Let us say that the bombs thrown contained an explosive newly discovered by the French, and of an extraordinary power of destruction. Some German *avions* made chase to the French *avions*, which were soon able to distance them without being touched by their projectiles. At 11.20 a.m. the *avions*, piloted by the Sous-Lieutenant Noël, arrived at Bukarest, where he descended directly in the aviation field, in the midst of the delirious acclamation of the Roumanian aviators. The biplane Lamprou descended at Alexandria, and the two others landed, according to orders, at Turnu-Magaurele.

Six hundred kilometres in a single stage! A hundred and twenty kilometres to the hour! The difficult crossing of the Balkans, with their heights of over 2,900 metres (9,000 feet), their pernicious currents, their thousand and one difficulties, effected without encumbrance, without the least accident! What marvellous exploit of ability, of cool blood, of this legendary and magnificent heroism French! What new and beautiful page of glory to inscribe to the credit of the aviation French! Salutes to you, glorious heroes of the air! Salutes to you, well-beloved colours of France, which in these solemn hours come to unite yourselves to the tricolour Roumanian! Roumania has received you open-armed with legitimate pride, and from the plains of the Danube up to the slopes of the Carpathians, and from the banks of the Olt and of the Muresh, and from those of the Black Sea, to those of the Thass, a sole cry sincere, but which sums up all our sentiments, will hail you, "*Vive la France! Vive l'armée française!!*"

High praise, very warmly expressed, and richly deserved!

One who writes with intimate knowledge of their movements, says:

The aviators deserved thoroughly the acclamation. All the French pilots remained for a while in Roumania except Louis Noël, who flew back alone on the nineteenth again without landing. Owing to a head wind after reaching the seaward side of the Balkans, he only just scraped home without a drop of essence.

It should be added that Lieutenant Noël is well known at Hendon, and has been justly termed one of the most decorated and distinguished of Hendon aviators.

FLIGHT-LIEUTENANT HAROLD ROSHER, R.N.A.S.

All are conscious of the fact that to our Royal Naval Air Service the highest praise is due. The service is rich in heroic pilots. Few, however, are known by name to the wider public. But we must not suppose that our navy has not in its service a goodly share of skilful and heroic pilots.

The letter, for instance, of Flight-Lieutenant Harold Rosher, R.N.A.S., written to his family and published by Chatto and Windus, reveals an aviator of fine character. A friend writes:

One wonders, whether most to admire the man in him, the gentleman, or the accomplished pilot of the skies who took all risks, keeping his head among them, because that way lay duty and achievement.

He is well reflected in his quiet, modest manner of writing. Here is a little picture of the difficulties of flying at a great altitude, 'absolutely lost' and in search of bearings:

I nose-dived, side-slipped, stalled, &c, &c, time after time, my speed varying from practically nothing to over a hundred miles an hour. I kept my head, but was absolutely scared stiff. I didn't get out of the clouds, which, lower down, turned into a snow-storm and hail, until I was only 1,500 feet up. I came out diving headlong for the earth.

Mastery of the air becomes still more difficult when making a raid, as Lieutenant Rosher did more than once, on the German fortifications along the Belgian coast. He writes:

A few seconds passed, and the shrapnel burst a good deal short of me, but direction and height perfect. I turned out to sea and put another two miles between me and the coast. By now a regular cannonade was going on. All along the coast the guns were firing hasty, vicious flashes, and then a puff of smoke as the shrapnel burst. I steered a zigzag course and made steadily to sea, climbing hard.

Of another time when he was under fire and travelling faster than he had ever travelled before, he writes:

My chief impressions were the great speed, the flaming bullets streaking by, the incessant rattle of the machine-gun and rifle fire, and one or two shells bursting close by, knocking my machine all sideways and pretty nearly deafening me.

There is inspiration in the letters, chiefly, perhaps, on account of the fact that they were written for the late Lieutenant Rosher's dearest friends. He was killed at Dover, while trying a doubtful machine before allowing a fellow-aviator to ascend—a hero's death.

He has been described as one of the most promising officers in the Service.

He was not merely a first-class pilot; he was a born organiser and leader of men, and, moreover, he had the heaven-sent gift of being personally popular with all ranks without losing his control over those below him.

Knowing personally all the senior officers under whom he served, they all had the highest regard for his personal qualities and for his ability as an officer.

A writer in the *Aeroplane* says:

One may deduce that his letters may fairly be taken as expressing the views, experiences, and feelings of the best class of R.N.A.S. officer, and his father, Mr. Frank Rosher, has done well in publishing them, for they give a vivid and intimate picture of life in the Royal Naval Air Service during the early days of the war. The naval censorship is to be congratulated on having left untouched certain passages which indicate to those who have understanding some of the mistakes made in those early days in the supply or choice of the engines, aeroplanes, and landing grounds. There is no grumbling in the letters themselves, but plain statements are set down.

The letters begin with Lieutenant Rosher's early experiences at the Bristol School at Brooklands, whither he went to learn as much as he could between applying for and receiving his commission, and the fact that he took this course is evidence of the keenness which in his short flying life carried him so far in the Service.

In one of his letters Lieutenant Rosher describes thus how he came through a curtain of fire:

I found myself across the yards and felt a mild sort of surprise. My eyes must have been sticking out of my head like a shrimp's! I know I was gasping for breath, and crouching down in the fuselage.

He was too brave a man to be afraid of admitting that he was afraid. Later in the book there is a story like a nightmare of how, when he went to attack an airship shed at Brussels, he was instead chased by a Zeppelin, which was already in the air when he got there, and so high up that his old machine could not reach it: the machine was, in fact, barely able to go fast enough to keep out of the way of the airship.

Lieutenant Kosher, although highly imaginative and impressionable, was, as we have seen, of the 'stuff' of which heroes are made. All who knew him join in acclaiming him a young officer of heroic mettle.

HEROES OF FRANCE

Vive la France! To her heroic sons we owe in a great measure the supremacy in the air enjoyed by the Allies. Who can forget the heroic and skilful M. Pégoud? Great is our debt to him. With his remarkable skill as a pilot in the earlier days of flying—his wonderful diving, 'turning and twisting,' his 'looping the loop' and flying upside down, all with amazing ease and grace—he taught the astonished world a great object-lesson in the materiality of the air.

He showed that the air can give the aviator as much support as water to a fancy swimmer, and that where stability is lacking the human brain can supply the need, and that in human flight, like the bird and its wings, the machine and the individual can be in closest touch.

To his bold example and skilful illustrations as a pilot we owe more than can be told. Above all, would we praise his heroic spirit.

It is indeed the heroic spirit of the airmen of France that has been largely the source of our great success. Who has not heard how at the time of the great German offensive against Verdun the aviators of France, thinking of naught but conquest for their beloved country, flew straight into enemy aircraft, thus robbing the enemy's pilots of their nerve, and gaining a supremacy by their self-sacrificing courage which has remained firmly in their grasp! And never must we forget that to the heroic courage of the airmen of France is added remarkable skill. Take, for instance, the triumphant French aviator Lieutenant Nungesser, who has brought down no less than twenty enemy machines. Such victories could only have been gained by great skill linked with indomitable courage.

The official *communiqués* of France tell many thrilling stories. Take, for instance, the following for September, 1916:—

★★★★★★★★★★★★★★★★

One of our aeroplanes, which was attacked by four enemy machines, succeeded in freeing itself from its opponents, one of which, subjected to machine-gun fire at very close quarters, fell in the Chaulnes district.

September 7.—Our *Service d'Aviation* took an active part in the actions of the past days on the Somme front, watching the movements of the enemy's infantry, carrying out bombardments in the rear of the German lines, and attacking with machine-guns troops on the march. Our machines, armed with guns, repeatedly bombarded the enemy's trenches. During the air-fights which took place yesterday two machines were brought down by our pilots. One fell in the direction of Gueudecourt, and the other in the neighbourhood of Brie-en-Santerre.

Five other German machines were forced to descend damaged.

During the night of the sixth, in spite of unfavourable atmospheric conditions, sixteen of our bombarding aeroplanes dropped heavy bombs on railway stations, bivouacs, and enemy stores at Roisel and Villecourt (Sommecourt), where a big fire was caused.

September 8.—Yesterday, on the Somme front, two enemy aeroplanes were brought down in the region of Epenancourt. Another was forced to land after a fight near our lines, and was destroyed by artillery fire.

★★★★★★★★★★★★★★★★

On the fifth day of the same month the champion French aviator of whom we have read, Lieutenant Guynemer, brought down in the region of Ablaincourt his fifteenth enemy aeroplane.

On September 10, 1916, French aeroplanes were engaged in forty actions over the enemy lines, in the course of which the German aircraft suffered appreciable losses. On the Somme front, Adjutant Dorme brought down his ninth aeroplane, which fell at Beaulencourt, south of Bapaume. Four other German machines fell damaged—one in the region of La Maisonette, the other to the north and the east of Péronne. On the Verdun front an enemy aeroplane which came under machine-gun fire at very short range crashed to the ground near Dieppe. Another machine was brought down in the German first lines near Vauquois.

On the following night French aeroplane squadrons dropped 480 bombs on the stations and enemy depots in the region of Chauny. Several machines belonging to this squadron twice flew from their aerodrome to the place where the bombardment was carried out. During the same night eighteen aeroplanes dropped numerous bombs on the military establishments at Ham and in the region to the south of Péronne.

The French aviator, Adjutant Maxime Lenoir, who distinguished himself at this time, calls for special note. On August 4, 1916, he brought down his sixth enemy machine, and performed other most valuable services. The coveted decoration, the Legion of Honour, has been conferred upon him.

Concerning French pilots in general, Mr. Lawrence Jarrold, writing in the *Daily Telegraph*, has said:

> In aviation, *les Boches n'existent plus,* everyone in this camp agrees. Since the Somme offensive no German aeroplane has ever dared to cross its own lines into French territory. The French have invented methods of air photography the perfection of which is almost miraculous. "Does not the enemy do the same?" I asked. "No, he never comes to photograph us, because we never let him." In July fifty-eight German aeroplanes were brought down by the French attacking squadron. One of the new French machines alone brought down seven Boches,

and not one of these machines was lost. These are the new attacking machines of extraordinary speed. There are other new
French aeroplanes of great power. Some of these have lost a
gunner killed, but all have always come back.

One of the French aviator-captains who showed me over the
camp was the officer who had himself read the letter taken
from a German aviator officer, moaning over the incompetency
of German aviation. That German aviation has ceased to count
on the Somme is no exaggeration at all. One morning I saw
over twenty French sausages lolling in the air, where they cast
a seeing eye upon the German positions. Not a single German sausage was anywhere to be seen—none has been seen for
weeks. "The moment a German sausage comes up, one of my
men rises and puts an inflammatory fuse into the thing, and it
bursts up," said the aviator-captain.'

Mr. Jarrold also reported that the same fate had befallen the German aeroplanes.

Not one dares cross over the lines. The result is that the German artilleryman is blind. He fires over and over again at the
same place upon which he had long ago trained his gun, but
he can fire nowhere else with any knowledge. French mastery
of the air on the Somme is an absolute fact. But in the air, on
the Somme, the Boches are now powerless, and the French
work their war machine absolutely peacefully. Their aviators
have told them that they are safe from air attacks, and they
know it is a fact.

On September 15 French aviators particularly distinguished themselves in combats above the enemy's lines on the Somme front. Sub-
Lieutenant Guynemer brought down his sixteenth, Sub-Lieutenant
Nungesser his twelfth, Lieutenant Heurtaux his sixth, and Sub-Lieutenant de Rothefort his sixth aeroplane. Moreover, it was confirmed
that, in one of the recent fights, Lieutenant Deullin secured his sixth
victory. Two other German machines, attacked at very short range,
were forced to descend in a seriously damaged condition. Moreover,
on the Verdun front, an enemy machine was brought down to the
north of Douaumont.

Bombarding aircraft showed great activity during the night of the
fourteenth. A squadron of ten machines dropped eighty-five bombs on
the railway stations and the lines at Tergnier and Chauny, and on the

station and the huts at Guiscard. Many of the bombs found their mark. A big fire was observed at Tergnier and the beginning of an outbreak at Guiscard. Another French squadron dropped forty bombs on the barracks at Stenay, where several fires were observed, and forty on the works at Rombach. One pilot got as far as Dillingen, in the Valley of the Saar, where he dropped eight bombs on a large workshop, causing a fire. During the same night the blast furnaces at Rombach received ten bombs, and the railway from Metz to Pont-a-Mousson four, which caused considerable damage. Later, it was learnt that besides the nine German aeroplanes brought down on the French front on the fifteenth, six other enemy machines were forced to come down in a damaged condition in their own lines after fights with French pilots.

On September 17 it was confirmed that an enemy machine, which was attacked by machine-gun fire by Adjutant Lenoir, fell north of Douaumont. This was the eighth brought down by this pilot. It was also confirmed that Adjutant Dorme defeated his tenth enemy machine, which fell on September 15 between Erie and Ennemain.

At a later date (September 23), French aviators fought fifty-six engagements on the Somme front, in the course of which four enemy machines were brought down, while four others were seen to fall in a damaged condition. During these fights Adjutant Dorme brought down his eleventh German machine (in the neighbourhood of Goyencourt), Lieutenant Deullin his seventh (south of Doingt), Adjutant Tarascon his sixth (south-west of Hergny). The fourth German machine reported as having been brought down fell south-west of Rocquigny. On the same day, in the region of Verdun, Adjutant Lenoir attacked a German machine at close quarters and brought it down in its lines north of Douaumont. This was the tenth machine brought down by Adjutant Lenoir.

At a later date, the French pilot, Adjutant Baron, accompanied by a bombardier, left his aviation camp at 7.15 p.m. and reached Ludwigshafen, in the Palatinate (about 100 miles from the nearest point of the French border), where three bombs were dropped on military establishments. Continuing their route, the aviators dropped three more bombs on an important factory at Mannheim (ten miles farther east), on the right bank of the Rhine, where a vast fire and several explosions were noticed. The aviators returned safely at 12.50 a.m.

On September 24, the German aviators having shown more activity than usual, French *escadrilles de chasse* delivered on the greater part of the front veritable aerial battles. French pilots gained great successes and indisputably had the upper hand of the enemy. On the Somme front there were twenty-nine engagements; four enemy aeroplanes were brought down. One fell in the Vaux woods. Two others successively attacked by Sous-Lieutenant Guynemer came down in flames after some minutes' fighting. Sous-Lieutenant Guynemer consequently brought down the same day his seventeenth and eighteenth aeroplanes.

The fourth machine fell south of Misery. Three other German machines were seriously hit and fell wrecked near Estrees; and in the region of Péronne four enemy machines were compelled to come to earth in their own lines. It is also confirmed that one of the German aeroplanes, given as seriously hit on September 22, was brought down between Misery and Villers-Carbonnel. Farther to the south, between Chaulnes and the Avre, six German machines were brought down. One of them fell in flames near Chaulnes, in the course of an engagement between four machines and a group of six enemy machines. The second fell at Licourt, the third at Parvillers, the fourth was seen crashing to earth south of Marchelepot, the fifth and sixth were brought down by the same pilot in an engagement between one of the French squadrons and six German aeroplanes, and they fell in the region of Andechy, one of them in the French lines.

In the region north of Chalons a Fokker fell in flames near the French lines, and another Fokker appeared to have been seriously hit. In the Verdun region an enemy aeroplane was fired at by machineguns at close quarters, side-slipped, and descended on the Poivre Hill. East of St. Mihiel a Fokker nose-dived into its own lines. In Lorraine a French pilot pursued a German machine for twenty kilometres (12½ miles) into its own lines, killed the passenger, and compelled the machine to descend. Another enemy machine came down in the Forest of Gamecy. Finally, in the Vosges, two enemy aeroplanes nose-dived into their own lines in an abnormal manner after fights with French pilots.

It is noteworthy that on the following morning Captain de Beauchamps and Lieutenant Daucourt, each piloting a machine, started at eleven o'clock from their aerodrome, and threw twelve bombs on the factories of Essen (Westphalia). The aviators returned safely to their landing-point after accomplishing a flight of 800 kilometres (500 miles)—a remarkable achievement! Captain de Beauchamps, who is twenty-nine years of age, once commanded a squadron on the Eastern frontier, and Lieutenant Guynemer served for some time under him. Lieutenant Daucourt, thirty-seven years old, also has many long-distance flights to his credit.

In April, 1913, he flew from Paris to Berlin, a distance of 560 miles, beating his own 'record' in the contest for the Pommery Cup, when he made the journey from Calais to Biarritz. In October of the same year, he started with a passenger for Cairo, a flight of 3,750 miles, but was forced to land in the Cilician Taurus, on November 26, owing to an accident. He has been mentioned in Army Orders for his fine courage and tenacity in the accomplishment of missions. In February, 1915, when attacked by two German aeroplanes and his machine-gun had jammed, he escaped by daring airmanship. In the following month he attacked four enemy machines singlehanded, and put them to flight.

Special reference must also be made to the heroic French aviator, Adjutant Tarascon, who was mentioned in the official *communiqué* of September 18 as having brought down five German aeroplanes. We learn from a French source that he enlisted voluntarily, having been rejected owing to an aviation accident, of which he was the victim, in peace time. He was picked up in a very serious state, and it was found necessary to amputate his left leg. Tarascon temporarily abandoned the sport which cost him this infirmity, but asked to be allowed to resume his position as pilot when it was a question of defending his country.

The courage of this hero cannot be sufficiently admired. He is an expert, and one would never believe, whilst watching the evolutions of the aeroplane which he handles with such skill, that he had but one leg. Recently, during one of these astonishing raids, almost level with the tops of the trees above the enemy lines, which have become a speciality of Allied aviation, Tarascon received a shell splinter in his artificial leg, the shot being so violent that the leg was broken.

A number of American volunteers are in the French Air Service. Inspired by the example of the heroic sons of the country they delight to serve, they have earned high honours and warm praise. Describing an action witnessed from an antiaircraft gun emplacement, one writer says:

> The Germans dropped back for a moment, then the whole force came forward to attack the Americans. There was a circular counter formation on the part of the Americans, and the rapid firing of the guns was accelerated. . . . At times it was impossible to distinguish the Germans from the Americans in this most unequal fight. We saw Prince and Balsley capsize and fall. In the apparent death-drop Prince righted his machine when near the ground, and returned to the aviation field uninjured,

but with a bullet through his helmet. Balsley was not so fortunate. He owes his life, perhaps, to the fact that his feet were strapped to the controls. An explosive bullet struck him on the hip, rendering him helpless for a time, but he was able to regain command of his machine sufficiently to make a landing, though the machine was completely wrecked.

Balsley explains that his machine-gun jammed during the second rush of the Germans. He is now in the American Ambulance Hospital in Paris. His wound is not believed to be dangerous, but the doctors say he will never fly again. Just after these two men had fallen, when things looked bad for the American squadron, reinforcements of French machines came up. The Germans were soon driven back across the lines, and the engagement was over. One German machine was destroyed and its two occupants killed, others were injured. The French suffered no casualties except the wounding of Balsley and the loss of his machine.

The American aviators are not reckless or foolhardy, but brilliant fliers, who use their heads. They continue to be very active, despite unfavourable circumstances, such as repeated bombardments of their camps and hangars by German aviators. The Germans try constantly to draw out the Americans. At Belfort they sought to get them at a disadvantage, and again just recently in a raid on Bar-le-Duc. In this latter engagement the Americans ascended as the invading squadron's approach was telephoned from the firing line. They met and opened fire directly over the French hangars at Bar-le-Duc.

The Germans again outnumbered them two to one. Both the French captain and Prince were forced to come down, one with a punctured gasoline tank, and the other with his ammunition box blown off by explosive bullets. Soon after Cowden's machine-gun choked, and he, too, descended, leaving Hall and Chapman to fight off the Germans alone until reinforced by a French squadron from Toul. They were then able to force the Germans back into German territory and inflict heavy losses, though no injuries were suffered on the French side.

Among the American aviators who have been most successful is Lieutenant Thaw. He has fought sixteen battles and brought down five adversaries. His machine received several bullets while over the

German lines at Verdun, one of which hit him in the elbow, breaking a small bone. He has recovered, and is again with the Corps. Sergeant Kiffin Rockwell destroyed a German 'plane on May 18, and attacked several on May 26, when he was badly wounded in the face. He brought down two German machines during the battle at Verdun. Sergeant Bert Hall, after a long, hard fight on May 22, brought down a German from a height of 13,000 feet. He followed it down 3,000 feet, and saw it crash to the ground just within the German lines.

On September 25, 1916, French *avions de chasse* fought forty-seven engagements on the Somme front. Five enemy machines were brought down, while three more, which were seriously damaged, were obliged to alight. Another machine, which was attacked at close quarters with a machine-gun, fell disabled, but could not be followed to the ground. During these engagements, Sous-Lieutenant Heurtaux brought down his eighth machine in the direction of Villers Carbonnel, and Adjutant Dorme his twelfth machine north of Lieramont. In the Woevre, Adjutant Lenoir attacked an enemy machine constructed to carry three, and after a very hard fight brought it down near Fromezey (north-west of Etain). This was the eleventh machine brought down by this pilot.

Further aerial combats, which again resulted in victory for the French aviators, were fought on September 27. Sous-Lieutenant Nungesser in the course of the day alone brought down two German aeroplanes between Le Transloy and Rocquigny, and an enemy captive balloon, which fell in flames in the Neuville district. These three victories bring up to seventeen the number of machines brought down by this pilot. Moreover, two other German aeroplanes which had been seriously hit fell out of control—one towards Le Transloy and the other near Le Mesnil Bruntel. Another captive balloon, attacked by French pilots, collapsed near Nurlu. In Champagne a Fokker, attacked at close quarters, fell at first in spirals, then vertically, and was smashed, crashing to the ground at Grateuil.

It is noteworthy that the much-vaunted German Fokker machine was now under the shadow of defeat. On September 27 a Fokker, on being attacked by a French pilot, crashed to the ground near Rheims. Another, shortly after, 'nose-dived' into its own lines. Many other German machines of the same type fell victims to the courageous and skilful French aviators. The French *communiqué* of September 24 recorded Lieutenant Guynemer's seventeenth and eighteenth victories over German aircraft on the Somme front. As a matter of fact,

Lieutenant Guynemer destroyed three aeroplanes on that day while extricating a brother aviator from the clutches of five enemy craft. Two of the latter took flight, and three remained. At 11.22 the first German was shot down. The second followed thirty seconds later, and the third, already in full flight, was destroyed at 11.25.

A summing up of the French *communiqués* issued between July 1 and September 25 showed that 250 enemy aeroplanes had been destroyed or brought down out of control within their own lines; twenty-two observation balloons had been burned; 142 objectives within the territory occupied by the Germans had been hit; and 5,426 bombs had been dropped. Such figures bear eloquent testimony to the air services of our gallant Allies.

Further good work was done in October of the same year. On the second day of the month Sergeant Sauvage brought down his fifth German machine. A few days later Adjutant-Pilot Baron and Adjutant Chazard bombarded at Stuttgart the Bosch magneto factory. Dense smoke was seen rising from this factory as the result of the bombardment. Stuttgart, the capital of Wurtemberg, is 100 miles from the nearest point on the French frontier. The return journey, therefore, involved a flight of at least 200 miles.

On the tenth day of the same month, in addition to numerous surveillance, reconnaissance, and range-regulating flights, French aeroplanes fought fifteen engagements in the Verdun region, fourteen south of the Somme, and forty-four north of that river. In the course of the latter engagements four enemy machines were brought down, one by Adjutant Dorme, who thus brought down his thirteenth machine. Six other enemy machines were seriously hit and fell into the German lines.

It is noteworthy, as showing the unity of action between the French and British Air Services, that on October 13 a Franco-British squadron of forty aeroplanes bombarded the Mauser Works at Oberndorf on the Neckar. Four thousand three hundred and forty kilogrammes (over four tons) weight of projectiles were dropped, and their attainment of the objectives aimed at was noted. Six German aeroplanes were brought down in the course of fights into which they entered to defend their factories. The raid on the Mauser factory was one of a series of attacks on important works in Germany carried out by Allied aviators. During the previous three weeks military establishments, blast furnaces, and factories had been raided.

A new method of warfare for aviators, first undertaken by French pilots, is that of flying low over the enemy's lines, and attacking enemy troops with machine-gun fire. The *Daily Telegraph* Paris correspondent, praising this work, has stated that:

> The aviators attached to the infantry belong to a special sec-
> tion. They precede each attacking wave by a few yards and fly
> extraordinarily low, sometimes not more than a hundred yards
> or so above the enemy's lines, upon which they drop bombs,
> thus paving the way for the infantry advance, and simultane-
> ously, of course, signalling back information to the infantry as
> it comes on.'

On October 22 it was reported that Adjutant Dorme had brought down his fifteenth machine at Barleux, and Marechal de Logis Fla-chaire his fifth machine, which was dashed to pieces on the ground in the same district. On the following day, in spite of a thick mist, French aircraft displayed activity and fought some twenty engagements. Three enemy machines were brought down—one to the north of Azannes, another near Ornes, while the third was seen to fall with a broken wing north of Romagne. Following upon an engagement fought by one of the French air squadrons with an enemy group in the region of Verdun, one of the French pilots came down to within about a hun-dred yards from the ground in order to set fire to a shed and to open with his machinegun on a motorcar.

Later it was reported that Sergt.-Aviator Sauvage had brought down his fifth German aeroplane. He was the youngest French aviator to be mentioned in dispatches. His one desire, we learn, since he was fourteen, was to become an aviator. At sixteen he was apprenticed to a small aeroplane builder. He worked hard, and under the direction of the aviator Gilbert he built a machine to which he added some small improvement. He had just gone to Valenciennes to try this machine when war broke out, and he had to make off, leaving the aeroplane behind, which presumably fell into the hands of the Germans. After one year of war, he managed to get taken into the aviation service, got his pilot's licence in March, and went to the front three months later.

It may be recorded here that a new name has been added to the official list of French aviators considered worthy of mention in dis-patches. This distinction is awarded only after an aviator has brought down his fifth enemy machine. At the time of writing (October, 1916), the following heroic French aviators enjoy this remarkable distinction: Sous-Lieutenant Guynemer, who has brought down eighteen enemy machines; Sous-Lieutenant Nungesser, seventeen; Adjutant Dorme, fifteen; Sous-Lieutenant Navarre, twelve; Adjutant Lenoir, eleven; Lieutenant Heurtaux, ten; Sergeant Chainat, nine; Lieutenant Deullin, eight; Sous-Lieutenant Chaput, eight; Sous-Lieutenant De la Tour, seven; Sous-Lieutenant Pégoud, six (killed in action); Sous-Lieutenant De Rochefort, six (killed in action); Adjutant Tarascon, six; Adjutant Bloch, Sergeant Viallet, Sergeant Sauvage, Adjutant Lufbery (American), and Marechal des Logis Flachaire, each five.

There can be no fitting praise in view of such achievements. Truly France has many heroic sons! Again, comes the cry—*Vive la France!*

AWARDS AND DECORATIONS

The various awards and decorations conferred upon aviators and other men of heroic stamp claim our keenest interest. Mention has already been made of the Victoria Cross and other familiar orders. Here we purpose setting down a few of the outstanding points of interest regarding leading French and Russian orders and decorations, and of certain medals awarded by our own king for heroic and meritorious service.

The Legion of Honour is the only *Order* of France. It was instituted by Napoleon in 1802 as a general military and civil order of merit. The French Cross of War dates from 1915, and is awarded for distinguished service to both officers and men. The qualification for the distinction is that the action must be mentioned in the orders of the day. The French military medal was created in 1852. N.C.O.'s and men are eligible. It is also deemed the highest decoration for generals.

The Russian Order of St. George was founded in 1769 by the Empress Catherine II. It was originally intended to be a reward for conspicuous bravery in the field. It consists of eight classes, the first four of which are higher degrees, and are awarded to officers only, the remaining four being reserved for men. The peculiar method of tying the ribbon of the order indicates the various classes.

The English Distinguished Conduct Medal was instituted in 1862, and is awarded for individual acts of distinguished conduct in the field. The Distinguished Service Medal was instituted in 1914, and is awarded to chief petty officers and men of the Navy, and non-commissioned officers and men of the Royal Marines in cases where the Distinguished Service Order would be inappropriate. The Distinguished Service Cross was originally the Conspicuous Service Cross instituted in 1901. In 1914 the title was changed to the Distinguished

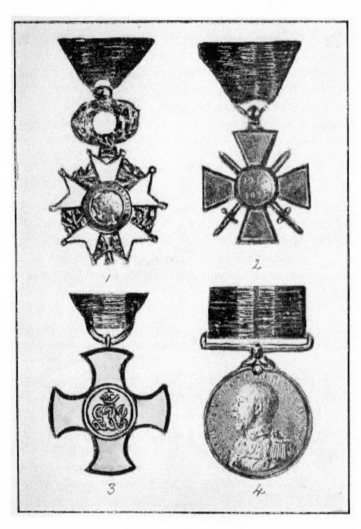

AWARDS AND DECORATIONS.

1. The Legion of Honour: Fifth Order, Croix Chevalier.
2. The French Cross of War.
3. The English Distinguished Service Cross.
4. Distinguished Service Medal.

Service Cross, and all officers below the rank of lieutenant-commander were made eligible for the award. It is frequently bestowed in cases where services are not considered of a suitable nature for appointment to the Distinguished Service Order.

We shall here see afresh how widely and how well awards and decorations have been earned by our airmen. Captain William Douglas Stock Sanday, M.C., R.F.C., has been made a Companion of the Distinguished Service Order for conspicuous gallantry and skill. He had led over thirty-five patrols with great courage. On one occasion a machine of his formation was attacked, but he charged and brought down the enemy machine in flames. He has destroyed at least four enemy machines.

The same honour has been conferred upon Lieutenant (temporary Captain) Alan Machin Wilkinson, for conspicuous gallantry and skill. He has shown great dash in attacking enemy machines, and up to the end of August, 1916, he had accounted for five. On one occasion while fighting a hostile machine he was attacked from behind, but out-manoeuvred the enemy and shot him down. Finally, he got back, his machine much damaged by machinegun fire.

The Military Cross has been awarded to Lieutenant (temporary Captain) Leslie Peech Aizlewood, for conspicuous gallantry and skill. Seeing five hostile machines, he manoeuvred to get between them and their lines; then, diving on one of them, he reserved his fire till he was only twenty yards off. The hostile machine fell out of control, but he was so close to it that he collided with it, breaking his propeller and damaging his machine. Though it was barely controllable, he managed to get back to our lines.

The same decoration has been conferred on Lieutenant (temporary Captain) John Oliver Andrews, for conspicuous gallantry and skill. He has proved a fine leader of offensive patrols, and has himself shot down four enemy machines. On one occasion he got within twenty-five yards of an enemy machine under heavy fire and brought it down a wreck.

The Military Cross has also been earned by Lieutenant (temporary Captain) Keith Riddell Binning, for conspicuous gallantry and skill, notably when he made two patrol flights over the enemy's trenches at a height of under 1,000 feet. His machine was repeatedly hit by machine-gun and rifle fire, but he rendered exact reports of the position of our own and the enemy's troops.

Lieutenant Allan Duncan Bell-Irving has also earned the Military

Cross for gallantry and skill in attacking a hostile balloon at 1,000 feet under heavy fire and bringing it down in flames. On a previous occasion he brought down a hostile machine.

Second-Lieutenant Walter Horace Carlyle Buntine is another recipient of the Military Cross. As escort to a bombing raid, he attacked several hostile machines, one of which fell to the ground nose first. Later he was attacked by three enemy machines, his own machine being damaged and himself severely wounded. With great skill he managed to land in our lines, though most of his propeller was shot away and his machine otherwise much damaged.

Second-Lieutenant Clifford Westley Busk has also been decorated with the Military Cross. He has taken part in many reconnaissances and fights, and on one occasion shot down an enemy aeroplane. On another occasion, when his pilot's control wires were cut and the machine went into a spin, he helped to restore stability by leaning far out on the upper side, and remained in this position till the machine got home.

Another officer in the R.F.C. to receive the Military Cross is lieutenant (temporary Captain) James Lander Chalmers. He has done much fine counter-battery work, often flying very low under heavy fire from the ground. On one occasion one of our shells broke the main spar of his machine. On another in one flight he dealt effectively with four enemy batteries.

It will be seen that the Military Cross is a much-favoured decoration for officers of the Royal Flying Corps. The deeds of gallantry and skill, however, for which the Cross has been awarded vary in many cases. Second-Lieutenant Leslie Frederick Forbes, has, for instance, been decorated for conspicuous gallantry and ability in attacking hostile machines and bombing railway lines, especially on one occasion, when he descended to 350 feet in order to accomplish his object. Second-Lieutenant Euan James Leslie Warren Gilchrist has also been decorated for conspicuous gallantry and skill when he attacked a hostile balloon and brought it down in flames, although under heavy fire and attacked by six hostile machines.

The case of Second-Lieutenant (temporary Captain) Ian Henry David Henderson is also worthy of special note. He drove down a machine out of control, and two days later dispersed six enemy machines which were attacking his formation. A few days later again he brought down an enemy biplane, the observer being apparently killed. A week after this he attacked and drove down another machine which had wounded his leader. He has also carried out several excellent contact patrols and attacked retiring artillery and a kite balloon.

Another heroic pilot (Second-Lieutenant Geoffrey Terence Roland Hill) attacked an enemy kite balloon under very difficult circumstances, and continued firing until he was within twenty feet of it. He was then only 1,000 feet from the ground and under heavy fire from anti-aircraft and machine-guns, but on looking round he saw the burning wreckage of the balloon on the ground. Mention must also be made of Captain Henry John Francis Hunter, who has done fine work for the artillery, and has accounted for many enemy guns. On one occasion, when a heavy storm drove all other machines back to their aerodromes, and the enemy guns took the opportunity to become active, he remained up and did excellent work.

Lieutenant (temporary Captain) Charles C. Miles has earned distinction for showing great dash in contact patrol work. On one occasion he reconnoitred an enemy trench at 500 feet altitude, under heavy fire, which severely damaged his machine. Five days later, while working at 600 feet, he was severely wounded.

On one occasion another heroic pilot, Captain Pearson, with one other pilot, attacked ten hostile aeroplanes. The other pilot had his controls cut and had to return, but Captain Pearson fought on till all the enemy aeroplanes were dispersed. On another occasion he bombed trains from a low altitude. He has done other fine work, and has been decorated by the King. Another pilot of similar stamp is Second-Lieutenant Herbert H. Turk, who, with Lieutenant Scott as observer, attacked seven hostile machines flying in formation. One was brought down as a wreck. When turning to meet another machine his rudder controls were shot away, and his machine got into a spinning nose-dive. After falling 5,000 feet he partially regained control, and, though his machine kept on turning, he managed to land safely. The machine was badly damaged; but, thanks to his skill, neither he nor his observer was hurt. He has been awarded the Military Cross.

Another to receive the Military Cross is Lieutenant John R. Philpott for conspicuous gallantry and skill in descending to about 300 feet, under heavy fire of all descriptions, in order to bomb a train. Finding that his fellow-officer, Captain Tyson, had wrecked the train, he dropped his bombs on a station and then assisted him to beat off hostile machines. He then, with Captain Tyson, attacked a machine which was endeavouring to leave the ground. He had previously displayed great gallantry.

In recognition of their gallantry and skill Captain J. Upton Kelly and Captain A. M. Miller have been made Companions of the Distinguished Service Order. Captain Kelly when making a reconnaissance came down to 700 feet under heavy fire, and obtained valuable information. Again, in attempting to observe through clouds, he flew over the enemy lines at 500 feet, and although severely wounded and almost blind, he brought his machine back to our lines. Captain Miller on one occasion flew close to the ground along a line of hostile machine-guns, engaging them with his machine-gun, drawing their fire, and enabling the cavalry to advance. Again, when alone, he engaged five enemy machines, bringing one down, and also successfully bombed a troop train, coming down to 300 feet to make sure of hitting.

Besides the names already given, the following officers have been awarded the Military Cross: Lieutenant Norman Brearley, Captain Dixon-Spain, Second-Lieutenant Spencer Reid. Each has performed remarkable feats. Lieutenant Brearley on one occasion went out to attack an enemy kite-balloon and managed to get immediately above his objective. He then pretended that he had been hit by antiaircraft fire and side slipped down to 1,500 feet, when he suddenly dived at the balloon, which was being hauled down, and fired into it until he almost touched it. When at 300 feet from the ground, the balloon burst into flames and was entirely destroyed.

Captain Dixon-Spain, with Second-Lieutenant Reid as pilot, attacked and drove back a hostile machine. A few minutes later four hostile machines were seen, three of which were attacked, one after another, and driven back, the fourth being accounted for by another patrol. Another time they attacked two hostile machines, shot one down, and drove the other back. Two days later they attacked two more machines, of which one is believed to have been destroyed, the other being pursued back to its aerodrome.

Reference must also be made of the courage and fortitude of Lieutenant Eardley Harper, who has been awarded the Military Cross for conspicuous skill in many aerial combats, and notably when his machine, with two others, met six hostile aeroplanes. He at once attacked, and shot down one machine. He then attacked and drove down a second one. A thick fog came on, and in landing his machine was wrecked, and he was badly cut and shaken. He managed, however, to walk two miles to his aerodrome and to deliver his report before collapsing. Another noteworthy case is that of Lieutenant Charles M. Chapman, who has been awarded the Military Cross for conspicuous skill in action against hostile aeroplanes. On one occasion he attacked three 'L.V' machines and one Fokker, shooting the latter down. Later, during an air battle with eleven enemy machines, he brought another Fokker down.

A GENERAL VIEW

The editor of *Flight* writes:

Any unbeliever in the reality of the command of the air being in the hands of Britain and her Allies,' must indeed be despaired of, after the daily records of the wonderful work of our pilots which are issued officially, combined with the unstinted *paeans* of praise emanating from every imaginable source upon this and the other side of the world.

Quite recently again, Mr. H. G. Wells repeated his admiration of the Allies' air-work; at the same time, he entered the lists with General Brussiloff as prophet as to the duration of the war, Mr. Wells putting it at June, 1917.' Mr. Wells' reasons for his prophecy are as follows:

I think so for a hundred reasons, but above all for these: The marvellous organisation of the French front, the mastery of the air which is assured to our aviators—I was witness of it, and I should rather say the exclusive possession of the air. Then the photographic marking by aeroplanes, in which the French take first rank. Lastly, by your artillery fire, which demolishes, methodically and mathematically the enemy batteries without fear of reprisals.

An interesting communication upon the same subject has just come to hand from the well-known correspondent of the *Chicago Daily News*, Mr. Edward Price Bell, in which he states that the British flying man is in the air every day between four and eight hours, constantly under fire. Ordinarily along the British front the flying men are in the air from two to three hours each day. Mr. Price Bell hits upon the basic reason for our superiority when he points out that our officers are always 'hunting for trouble' above the German lines, never declining a combat, and fighting, however outnumbered. Altogether he calculates that up to the latter part of 1916 British flying men on the Western front must have flown entirely over the enemy's fines much more than a million miles.

An officer of the Royal Flying Corps, also writing of the supremacy of the Allies, says:

Man for man, we undoubtedly are masters of the air on the west front. This fact I attribute to the mental and physical training we give our boys in England. Our youngest pilots have done wonderfully well. They learn quickly, are intensely keen, have great alertness of mind and act instinctively.

Another adds:

Our people have the tails up morally and mechanically, and though they have plenty of fighting when they get to the other side of the Hues, they are on the offensive all the time. The moral as well as the physical uplift is considerable, when one has a machine which will get above the German range of accurate fire in a quarter of an hour, and will do in or about 100 miles an hour when pushed. With such a machine one can attack and keep on attacking; and though perhaps not even the majority of our people are mounted on such machines, the worst machine at the front today is probably nearly as good as the best a year ago, and there are enough of the first-class machines to protect the weaker brethren. Despite all the errors of the past, our air service has certainly acquired dominance, if not absolute command, in the air, and for that fact very great credit is due to the officers who have so thoroughly reorganised affairs at the War Office, and who have so notably increased the performance and output of the machines now in use.

The great improvement in the construction of machines for long-distance flying is particularly worthy of note. We have seen how Captain de Beauchamps, leaving France in the morning, flew in broad daylight as far as Munich, where he dropped bombs on the stations. Then turning at right angles towards the south, he flew over the whole of the Tyrol and crossed the Alps, to land at length 12½ miles north of Venice, in the village of Santa Dona, on the small River Piave, having journeyed without stopping a distance of about 700 kilometres.

Captain de Beauchamps holds the flight record for bombing raids on German towns, but the longest journey made by an Allied aviator during the war was that of Lieutenant Marchal, who visited Berlin on a previous date. He, however, only dropped pamphlets on the German capital, before making off to the Russian frontier. He came down sixty miles within the German lines, having flown over 800 miles.

Captain de Beauchamps was accompanied in his great flight to Essen by Lieut. Daucourt, who made at the time some extremely interesting entries in his logbook:—

★★★★★★★★★★★★★★★★★

11 a.m. My friend Beauchamps has just gone, and I followed two minutes later. One thousand yards up, 2,000–3,000, we keep on getting higher and higher. The weather is clear with just a few clouds over 9,000 feet. The air is distinctly cold.

12 a.m. I am full over the Boche lines. We are seen and the anti-aircraft guns start a curtain fire a little forward but too high. The white puffs of the 77 make a line of smoke which I have got to cross. Soon the shots become more and more numerous; 300 shots at least must have been fired in a few minutes. Time after time I get right into the smoke of the bursting shells, and I can hear pieces of steel whistle near, very near. Oh! the Boche gunner rectifies his range. But he is too low now, so I go higher still, and I pass . . . Now there are shots on my left, which burst with black smoke, 105 calibre shells.

This is getting more serious. Shots get nearer, I point towards the left slightly, and, all of a sudden, I go ninety degrees to the left and drop straight towards the ground for 300 feet. The game is finished and the gunners done. Out of spite they shoot all over the place, and the shells burst now at the back of me. It looks as if I was going to get out of trouble without much difficulty . . . Now where is my friend? I cannot see him. Has he been brought down? Has he changed his line? A little under me I can see a big, fat yellow 'plane. Black crosses! It's a Boche. Another one follows very near.

The distance between us is about 600 feet, but they are slower than I am. *Clac—clac—clac.* It is Mr. Boche opening fire. The short bursts of his machine-gun keep crepitating. The brute does not shoot badly. Shall I engage him in a fight? It is really very tempting. But no, Essen is my only target, and I have no right to compromise, by a passing engagement, the success of our raid. I open my engine right out, and soon lose my aggressors. . . . As I fly over Treves I just distinguished on my left the outline of another 'plane. It is getting nearer and nearer. The sun prevents me from seeing it clearly, although I seem to recognise the silhouette of my companion's machine. No doubt it is he. I can now see his blue, white and red cocarde. And all of a sudden, I feel very happy . . .

A little later I change my direction and go straight north, leaving Coblenz on my left. Far in front of me I can see a small grey ribbon . . . The Rhine. It looks beautiful from up here. Somehow my confidence

187

increases every minute. Sure, everything will go well. I cross over the right bank. On the river many long convoys of barges go up towards Coblenz. If only I did not have a consignment of bombs to deliver, I should go down to gun them. It is funny how strong these temptations are. . . . Here is Bonn. My friend and co-raider is still on my right. My engine keeps on turning merrily, and I marvel at the ease with which I have covered these first 200 kilometres. A quick calculation shows me that we are going at the rate of about 130 miles an hour. It is a goodish speed. The weather is cold up here. My thermometer shows sixteen degrees below zero. To try and get warm I move arms and legs as much as I can in that cramped space. A few drops of peppermint which I drink warm my inside and cool my mouth . . . Underneath the Rhine, and still more boats! . . . Now we pass a town which seems enormous.

It is Cologne. What a splendid target it would make! But there are women, children, old people, and I am a soldier, not a pirate. I must only aim at destroying the military power of the enemy. Now I point straight towards Dusseldorf. But all the district disappears under a pool of smoke. What an extraordinary agglomeration of works! Here are Solingen, Elberfeld, Barmen, black country criss-crossed by innumerable railway lines and with hundreds of high chimneys, like guns, pointing to the sky. Down there a tremendous amount of arms of all sorts, guns, munitions, &c, all to be directed against us, are produced with a tremendous activity.

Essen at last. I am over what has been considered as the heart of Germany, over the town which stands as the symbol of brutal force. Where now are the Krupp's works? There, at the west of the town. How large they are! The shops and buildings, between which trains are running, seem innumerable. The attempts to disguise it are indeed foolish. It is the most perfect target one can imagine. Now I suppose I am going to be *strafed*. I look here and there for bursting shells. Nothing! They aim too low. However, some very violent waves of air of which I do not understand the cause disturb for a moment my bombing preparations.

2 o'clock. The centre of the works pass. I drop my torpedoes in rapid succession. My friend, who is over me and a little on the left, drops his also. I guess, more than I can exactly see, as I am so very high, that underneath in the works the people suffer from a sort of madness. There are rushes of people soon hidden by clouds of smoke which rise from many points.

Nearly at the centre it seems that there is a formidable explosion, followed by intense fire. What a joy to have attained one's aim! Krupp has been bombed, in full daylight, in spite of its anti-aircraft guns and of its 'planes. I suppose that now the Boches must be mad with fury, and will try to chase us. Never mind, my mission has been fulfilled. I will fight enemy 'planes if they come ... Here I am again over Dusseldorf, but not going so fast as in coming. The wind, which has veered, hampers me. A quick verification of my oil and petrol tanks. All is well; I can keep up for another six hours. The clouds get denser and denser. There is at some moments a thick mist, which veils completely the ground.

As I am browsing, some explosions thunder louder than the noise of my engine. I turn right round, so that the Boche gunner loses the range. But as I turn, I see 1,500 or 2,000 feet under me three Boche 'planes who are giving chase. Their machines are as fast as mine, but as soon as they try to go up, they lose ground. I slacken for a few seconds, and going straight towards the most forward of them, I serve him at about 150 yards with three bursts of my machinegun. Unnerved, he prefers not to engage a fight and flies towards the left. But the others are attacking me from the back. It is time to go ... Have I wounded my opponent? I don't think so, as he seems to be flying straight again, but very much lower.

Soon the two others are only black spots ... The chase has lasted over thirty minutes, and I have got a real stiff neck, so often did I turn round ... Now I have been up six hours. Time drags dreadfully. My eyes hurt, and I suffer from the cold. Evidently, I am over Belgium now. But where? I must know. I come down, engine stopped. How sweet is that silence, after six hours of tempest! Four thousand feet; it is low enough.

6.30. I cannot stand it anymore, I am coming down, 7,000 feet, 5,000 feet, 1,000 feet. I cannot hear the guns any more. But what are these? Bivouacs. Am I in France? I keep on for another quarter of an hour, going south, and finally alight in an immense field, far from a village. If I am on the territory invaded by the Germans I'll fly away under their nose. I am at the end of the field, ready to start again in case of need. I have kept my engine turning slowly. After five minutes of waiting, some people come running towards me—peasants. I shout to them at the top of my voice, "Where am I?" "At Champaubert," they answer me. What a joy is mine! I am in France. Back, after having succeeded in what seemed to men an impossible enterprise.

It is particularly interesting to note that in their remarkable flight both Captain de Beauchamps and Lieutenant Daucourt used machines of British manufacture.

We have seen that the officers and men of the Royal Naval Air Service have also to their credit many long-distance flights. Indeed, in all respects the R.N.A.S. have kept at 'level-fight' with the R.F.C. The two Services work, however, under different conditions. The following is an extract from a report from Admiral Sir John R. Jellicoe, G.C.B., G.C.V.O., then Commander-in-Chief, Grand Fleet:

> *Iron Duke*, August 23, 1916. Sir,—With reference to my dispatch of June 24, 1916, I have the honour to bring to the notice of the Lords Commissioners of the Admiralty the names of officers who are recommended for honours and special commendation. Where all carried out their duties so well it is somewhat invidious and difficult to select officers for special recognition.

We have seen, however, that many naval aviators have been decorated. In addition to the names already given, mention must be made of Flight-Lieutenant F. J. Rutland, who has been decorated with the Distinguished Service Order for his gallantry and persistence in flying within close range of four enemy light cruisers, in order to enable accurate information to be obtained and transmitted concerning them. Conditions at the time made low flying necessary.

This is also a fitting place to record that it has been officially announced that the King has conferred the Distinguished Service Cross on Flight-Lieutenant Charles T. Freeman, R.N.A.S., for the following act of gallantry: On the night of August 2, 1916, he made a determined attack on a Zeppelin at sea, only abandoning the attack when he had exhausted all his ammunition. As darkness was approaching at the time, and his chances of being picked up were problematical, his courage and devotion in returning to the attack a second and third time were exemplary.

There is every indication that our airmen are becoming more heroic and skilful each passing day. Touching their great service in dealing with enemy airships, the editor of the *Aeroplane* writes:—

★★★★★★★★★★★★★★★★★

One of the commonest and cheapest jeers of certain papers which have adopted anti-Churchillism as part of their political creed has been the constant jibe at the late First Lord of the Admiralty that the defence which he promised against enemy airships has not been forthcoming. It is now many, many months—in fact, it runs into years—since Mr. Winston Churchill informed the world that, if enemy airships ventured to invade this country, they would be met by "a swarm of hornets" which would make them regret that they had ever come.

At that time the defence of England was entirely in the hands of the navy. The army was still piously supposed to be the Expeditionary Force. Naturally, as part of the Navy, the R.N.A.S. was supposed to be responsible for the defence of the country against aircraft; a perfectly logical position, and an eminently sensible one, for the Navy has always been able to obtain all the money it has wanted for any scheme it might have in hand. Consequently, there seemed to be no reason why Mr. Churchill's rhetorical phrase—to which one might have returned the time-honoured question, "Is that a threat or a promise?"—should not have become before long a literal truth.

There was one point on which all of us seem to have tripped up, however—namely, that in talking or thinking of invasion by aircraft we all pictured to ourselves a fleet of machines coming over in broad daylight, and the world's aerial navies grappling in full sight, complete with central blue as fitted. None of us seems to have had the sense to see that nocturnal invasions would be very much more effective, both morally and practically, than any daylight show could have been.

If the Germans had sent their airships over early in 1915, in daylight, they would certainly have been wiped out by aeroplanes. We had very few aeroplanes then; not a fraction of the number we should have had if the supply of engines and machines had been properly handled before the war by the Government. But nevertheless, we had some few, such as Sopwith tabloids and Bristol scouts, quite capable of reaching and catching and destroying any airship of that period, if it could be seen. The destruction of the very first Zeppelin ever brought down by an aeroplane—that which ultimately wrecked itself after being damaged and made uncontrollable by Squadron-Commander Bigsworth, R.N.—proves it, for this officer was flying a standard 80 h.p. Avro, a considerably slower machine than either of the single-seaters mentioned. The Germans spotted this quickly enough, and so their ships only came over at night, with the result that for over a year they came and went unhindered, so far as defensive aeroplanes were concerned. The only people who suffered were the gallant young officers of the R.N.A.S., who went up to try to abolish the airships.

The Admiralty published openly the names of those killed in these operations. Young Mr. Lord, of Newcastle, was, I believe, the first victim. He was killed in the south of England when trying to land a fast scout in the dark. Much about the same time Mr. Hilliard was killed through the bombs he had on board his Caudron exploding as he landed. Mr. Richard Gates was killed when landing a Henry Farman in the dark. Mr. Barnes was killed through landing a big Sopwith pusher in the early morning fog after flying all night. There may have been other deaths, but those are all I recall in the early part of 1915.

There were many other officers injured, and still many more marvellous escapes. I have been told how an officer jumped out of his machine near the ground, chancing where he fell rather than risk being blown up by his bombs. Another officer had a still more extraordinary experience. He landed on a Caudron, and his bombs blew up. Subsequently investigation showed clearly where his skids first struck the ground. About twenty-five yards farther on was the wreck of the machine and engine, all burnt to bits by the petrol set on fire by the bombs; and about twenty yards farther still was the place where the pilot had finished having a private fire of his own.

Seemingly the first shock had jarred and bent the stems of the bombs and released the firing mechanism. The second shock had exploded them, had blown the whole machine to pieces, had burst the petrol tank so that the spirit splashed all over the pilot and caught light, and, finally and fortunately, had blown the pilot clean out of the machine into some longish grass, where he fell without being stunned, and rolled over and over till he put the flames out. I gather that his worst injury was a rather burned hand, due to his glove falling off while he was beating the flames out on his coat.

★★★★★★★★★★★★★★★★★

Never must we forget the debt we owe to these heroes of the Royal Naval Air Service. They have played, as we have seen, a most heroic part. And we would bear in mind the fact that the work of our heroic aviators covers the *whole* field of the World War. In Mesopotamia, for instance, much good work has been done. A correspondent of the *Daily Telegraph* wrote in October, 1916:

> On the night of the 19th one of our aeroplanes raided an enemy aerodrome at Shumran, dropping eight 20-pound bombs, which fell all round a machine, apparently damaging the same, and putting out lanterns left on the ground by the guard, who

fled on the aviator's approach. Early in the morning of the 26th two of our aeroplanes successfully bombed a hangar, descending to 100 feet. One of our machines was damaged. A bullet cut a control wire, and the aeroplane "nose-dipped" 1,000 yards, but the pilot succeeded in righting the machine and landed safely. The Turks, believing they had destroyed the machine, started cheering in the trenches. Several exposed themselves, and were "picked off."

At a later date news came from Mesopotamia of an affair which afforded a striking instance of aeroplanes working in co-operation with cavalry. Mounted enemy irregulars had driven off our camels on the left bank of the river, and were proceeding north-west. Two aeroplanes were sent out with machine-guns to attack the raiders. Our aviators soon passed over scattered bodies of mounted men, who were taking cover in *nullahs* and firing at the machines. These were driven out by machine-gun fire from the aeroplanes, and, breaking into small groups, made for the hills. Several were hit, and three or four killed. During the action our machines flew very low, descending at times to within twenty feet of the ground.

After dispersing this body our aviators pursued the raided camels, which were seen being driven towards the hills by troops of irregular cavalry. Fire was opened from the aeroplanes, and the escort immediately abandoned the camels, retiring towards the mountains. A troop of our cavalry coming up recaptured the camels. The machines and cavalry continued to chase the raiders, inflicting further casualties.

Further reports from the same quarter show that on October 25, 1916, one of our aviators, returning from a reconnaissance, attacked a party of enemy irregular cavalry. After dropping bombs among them, he descended to 800 feet, firing his machinegun into them, and killing many. In the evening five of our machines raided a cavalry camp by Shattlhai, dropped bombs, and again brought the machine-gun into action, causing considerable loss and panic.

All will remember how our aviators, overcoming many serious difficulties, dropped provisions into besieged Kut, thus enabling our soldiers to prolong their defence.

In Egypt also some very useful work has been done. The Officer Commanding has reported that on September 4, 1916, the Royal Flying Corps carried out a further raid on the enemy's encampment at Mazar. One anti-aircraft gun was put out of action and a number of bombs were dropped with good effect on camps, supply depots, and camel lines. Further reports showed that on the following day two of our aeroplanes raided the Turkish aerodrome and aeroplane repair section at El Arish. Twelve bombs were dropped with good results. Enemy aeroplanes attacked our machines, but did not close, and only opened fire at long range. They ultimately gave up the fight, and our machines returned undamaged.

From Salonika news came in September, 1916, of an enemy machine being shot down on the seventh and of a second enemy machine being shot down on the following day north-east of Lake Doiran. The days that followed were equally favourable to the Allied airmen. An account of the sensational landing of a French bombarding aeroplane containing two aviators has come from an officer in the Doiran district:

> A piece of bursting shrapnel having severed one of the control wires of an aeroplane, the machine began to dive head-foremost and was apparently lost. It was falling within the enemy's lines, to the great delight of the Bulgarians. When within a hundred yards of the ground the observer managed to leave his seat, and succeeded in hoisting himself on to the upper plane of his machine, where, lying on the canvas, he was able to restore the balance of the machine by moving the plane by hand. The motor controls were undamaged, and as soon as the equilibrium of the aeroplane was restored it was able to return to the Allied lines and land without further mishap, with a bomb still on board.

Another sensational incident was that of a naval observer in a 'sausage' balloon operating in Macedonia, attacked by two Fokkers, which fired a stream of bullets, piercing the 'sausage' at several points and destroying the telephone. The observer had on board a small machine-gun and a parachute. After having sent the contents of two belts of ammunition at his enemies, the gun jammed. He then threw himself overboard with his parachute, and fell for about 600 feet. At last, however, the parachute opened, and the observer landed safely. After which the balloon was repaired and he went up again.

From the Secretary of State for India news came in November, 1916, of aeroplanes being used in Indian warfare for the first time. Large Mohmand forces (estimated at 6,000) collected on the border opposite Shubkadr, and were dealt with by our aviators with remarkable effect.

Each passing day our heroic airmen add to their laurels. But it must not be supposed that so much has been accomplished without the loss of valuable lives. Many heroic men—aviators of whom we are prouder than words can tell—have made the supreme sacrifice.

THE HEROIC DEAD

The author of *The Wrack of the Storm* says:

Those who die for their country, must not be numbered with the dead . . . This death, on the field of battle, in the clash of glory, becomes more beautiful than birth, and exhales a grace greater than that of love. No life will ever give what their youth is offering us, that youth that gives, in one moment, the days and the years that lay before it. There is no sacrifice to be compared with that which they have made; for which reason there is no glory that can soar so high as theirs, no gratitude that can surpass the gratitude which we owe them. They have not only a right to the foremost place in our memories: they have a right to all our memories and to everything that we are, since we exist only through them.

Amongst the heroic aviators who have made the supreme sacrifice is Lieutenant William Herbert Stuart Garnett, R.F.C., who was killed while making a flight. While still at the university, Mr, Garnett, who in 1903 took a First Class in the Mechanical Science Tripos, wrote a book on the turbine engine, which went through several editions, and was translated into German. After a brief spell as a master at Eton, he was called to the Bar, and though he did not practise, he produced a valuable book on *Children and the Law*. Mr. Garnett had made a special study of the National Insurance Act, and joined the legal department of the Commission when it was set up. On the outbreak of war, he joined the R.N.V.R., and did valuable work in mine-sweeping for nearly a year. He was a son of Dr. William Garnett, the eminent educationalist.

Many other men of high promise have made the great sacrifice. Captain Keith Lucas, R.F.C, who was killed in a flying accident on October 5, 1916, had already acquired a world-wide reputation as one of the most promising physiologists of the younger generation. Captain Lucas was born in 1879, was the son of Francis Robert Lucas, and was educated at Rugby and Trinity College, Cambridge, of which he became a Fellow in 1904. He was elected F.R.S. in 1913, and was invited to give the Croonian lecture to the Royal Society even a year before his election to it. Before the war he was fully engaged in both teaching and research work at Cambridge, and was, moreover, one of the directors of the Cambridge Scientific Instrument Company. But on the outbreak of war all this was put aside in order that he might devote his rare instrumental skill and inventiveness to the Flying Services.

Lieutenant Anderson Mann, R.F.C, who lost his life whilst on active service on August 9, 1916, was twenty-one years of age, and was educated at Ardvreck, Charterhouse and Trinity College, Cambridge. Mr. Mann was the best rifle shot of his year in the Public Schools. On the outbreak of war, he was gazetted to the Scottish Rifles, and joined the R.F.C. in March last. Shortly afterwards he and his pilot distinguished themselves by bringing down eight German aeroplanes in seven days. They were each awarded the Military Cross for consistent gallantry and skill. Mr. Mann was the eldest son of Mr. John Mann, chartered accountant, of Glasgow and London.

Captain Leslie Charles, R.F.C, who was killed in action on July 30, 1916, was the second son of Mr. and Mrs. R. Stafford Charles, of Broomfield, Stanmore. He was educated at Stanmore Park, where he took a Mathematical Scholarship for Harrow. At Harrow he became a member of the O.T.C. and the Philatelic Club, and was also head of his house. He left Harrow in July, 1914, and in the following month received a commission in the Worcestershire Regiment. In May, 1915, he was sent to Gallipoli, and was present at the battles of June 4-9. He was subsequently invalided home, and was gazetted Captain on November 20, 1915. Early in 1916 he joined the R.F.C., and took his pilot's certificate in April. He left for active service on July 5 and lost his life in a combat in the air over the German lines.

Second-Lieutenant J. Hampson Dodgshon, who lost his life on October 1, 1916, at the age of twenty-five, was educated at Westminster, and was a member of the school cadet corps. He joined the H.A.C. in July, 1913, and played Rugby Football for the corps. He went abroad with the H.A.C. in September, 1914, and spent the first winter of the war fighting in Flanders and France. He was invalided home, and on his recovery was gazetted to a commission in the Surrey Yeomanry. He served for six months in Egypt, and was at the Dardanelles as Assistant Military Landing Officer. On his return to England, he declined a post as Assistant Equipment Officer in the R.F.C., as he felt he ought to take a more active part in the war. He obtained his 'wings' in August, and was made an instructor. His commanding officer writes of him: 'His memory will be green for ever.'

Captain Brooke-Murray, another heroic officer to lose his life in action, was educated at Cheltenham College. At school he was a very good shot, and was in the Cheltenham Bisley Eight of 1908, 1909, and 1910. Entering Sandhurst in September, 1910, he was gazetted to the A.S.C. in 1911. He went to France in August, 1914, with the first Expeditionary Force, and took part in all the operations of the 19th Brigade from Mons to the Marne and Aisne, Ypres and Armentieres. From April to July, 1915, he was adjutant of the advanced Horse Transport, and from July to October, 1915, he was staff captain, G.H.Q. Afterwards he became embarkation officer, Marseilles, and officer to the Divisional Ammunition Park (April to June, 1916). He was then flying officer observer to the date of his death from wounds received in action on September 16 in an air combat against three enemy aviators.

The Royal Naval Air Service has lost a valuable officer by the death in a flying accident of Squadron-Commander Dalrymple Clarke. Before joining the R.N.A.S., in 1913, he was in business in London, and prior to that he was an officer of cavalry. After joining the R.N.A.S., he was stationed for some time at Eastchurch, and quickly showed that he was not only a very fine pilot, but had the gift of studying his machine's peculiarities and reporting thereon in a manner which made his tests of high value to the Service.

From Eastchurch he was transferred to the Central Flying School, under Commodore (then Captain) Godfrey Paine, R.N., and was appointed an instructor. There he did much useful work, and was responsible for the training of many pilots who have since distinguished themselves on active service. Later on, he was appointed to experimental work, and carried out many tests which produced far-reaching results, not only as regards aeroplanes, but also concerning engines, bomb-dropping, and various scientific adjuncts to aircraft.

Another loss to the Royal Naval Air Service and the country came with the death of Flight-Lieutenant Charles Walter Graham, R.N., D.S.O., who was awarded the D.S.O. for his services on December 14, 1915, when, with Flight-Sub-Lieutenant A. S. Ince as observer and gunner, he attacked and destroyed a German seaplane off the Belgian coast.

The Royal Flying Corps lost another most promising officer with the death in action of Captain J. 0. Cooper, R.F.C., previously reported missing, now stated to have fallen in action. He was twenty years of age, and was the youngest son of Lady Cooper, of Ossemsley Manor, Christchurch, Hampshire. Educated at Lockers Park and Harrow, he returned from Australia for the war. He joined the R.F.C. and got his commission in January, 1915. Captain Cooper was considered by all who knew him one of the most promising men in the R.F.C, and if he, had been spared would, it is said, have led a squadron before he was twenty-one.

Further loss came with the death in action of Lieutenant Ian Macdonnell, R.F.C. He obtained his brevet from the Royal Aero Club as a pilot in December, 1913, after passing through the Bristol School of Flying at Brooklands. Soon after the outbreak of war he was gazetted a lieutenant in his father's regiment, Lord Strathcona's Horse. In March, 1915, he became A.D.C. to Brigadier-General J. E. B. Seely, C.B., D.S.Q., commanding the Canadian Cavalry Brigade, and served with them in the trenches, including the Battle of Festubert, till he became attached, on probation, to the R.F.C. in September, 1915. He was gazetted flying officer on November 6 of the same year. He met with a serious accident through the failure of his engine in December, 1915. His observer was killed and he himself more or less seriously injured. He reported for duty with the R.F.C. on May 18, 1916. His major in the R.F.C. wrote that he was very skilful, full of daring and gallantry. He was a grandson of Lieutenant-Colonel J. T. Campbell, a Crimean veteran, and his father belonged to a Cadet family of the Macdonnells of Glengarry, which have given so many officers to the Empire.

In the case of another gallant officer, Second-Lieutenant L. C. Kidd, death followed quickly upon brilliant achievements. Shortly before his death he was awarded the Military Cross. He took his pilot's certificate at Hendon before the war, and was tea-planting in Ceylon when war was declared. He returned as soon as possible, and was at once given a commission in the R.F.C., and, after a short period of home training, went to the front in February, 1916. Since then, with two short intervals of leave, he had been flying continuously at the front.

Amongst other names on the Roll of Honour we would mention Second-Lieutenant J. S. Mitchell, Second-Lieutenant Aubrey F. A. Patterson, Second-Lieutenant Robert Shirley Osmaston, M.C., and Lieutenant Edward Carre.

Second-Lieutenant J. S. Mitchell, R.F.C., was the only son of Colonel and Mrs. Mitchell, of Sandygate, Wath-on-Dearne, Rotherham. He was educated at Bramcote School, Scarborough, and Rugby, leaving there in July, 1914. He went for a tour to Australia and Canada, returning in July, 1915, when he began to work on munitions at Sheffield. In January, 1916, he applied for a commission in the R.F.C., and was gazetted in June, being appointed a Flying Officer on September 4. He died abroad of injuries accidentally received on October 5, aged twenty.

Second-Lieutenant Aubrey F. A. Patterson, R.F.C., who is unofficially reported as having died of wounds while a prisoner of war in Germany, was born in 1895. He was the youngest son of Mr. and Mrs. W. R. Patterson, of 40 Cleveland Square, Hyde Park. Educated at Berkhamsted and Eastbourne College, he distinguished himself as an athlete, and won the swimming championship at Eastbourne when he was sixteen. Within a few days of the commencement of the war he enlisted in the H.A.C., and went out to France at the end of 1914. Returning invalided to England in 1915, he was appointed to a commission in the West Yorkshire Regiment, and was subsequently attached to the R.F.C. He went back to the front in 1916, and became actively engaged in bombing operations, in which he did 'excellent work'. He was brought down on September 17 by a numerous German squadron, and died of his wounds at Osnabrück.

Second-Lieutenant Robert Shirley Osmaston, M.C., was the son of Mr. and Mrs. Francis P. Osmaston, of Stoneshill, Limpsfield, and grandson of Mr. John Osmaston, late of Osmaston Manor, Derby. He was born in 1894, and educated at Earleywood Preparatory School, Ascot, and Winchester College (Kingsgate House), where he gained the gold medal for gymnastics in 1912. He had a short course of agricultural training after leaving Winchester, and when the war broke out enlisted as a private in the U.P.S. Brigade. In May, 1915, he obtained his commission in the Royal Sussex Regiment, and went to the front on December 1, 1915. Early this year (1916) he was an instructor of Lewis gun training, and later acting-adjutant of his brigade, and was attached to brigade headquarters learning staff work. In April he conducted a raid into the enemy trenches very successfully and without any casualties, and was shortly afterwards awarded the Military Cross. In July he transferred to the R.F.C., and served as observer till he was killed.

Lieutenant Edward Mervyn Carre, R.F.C., who was killed in October, 1916, aged twenty-two, was the youngest son of the Rev. Arthur A. Carre and Mrs. Carre, of the Rectory, Smarden, Kent. Educated at Christ's Hospital from 1903 to 1910, he left as Deputy Grecian and entered the College of the Resurrection, Mirfield, and in 1912 matriculated at Leeds University, whence he obtained an Honour Degree in Classics. On the outbreak of war, he joined the Artists' Rifles, and served abroad, receiving a commission in the Lincolnshire Regiment in March, 1915. Being promoted Lieutenant, he was transferred to the R.F.C. in May, 1916. His commanding officer writes:

We are all very sorry to lose your son. He has done very good work since joining the squadron, and was really one of my best observers.

His eldest brother, Maurice Tennant Carre, Australian Infantry, was killed at Lone Pine on September 2, 1915. Two remaining brothers, Captain M. H. Carre, M.C., and Second-Lieutenant G. T. Carre, are serving in the Royal West Kent Regiment, and have both been twice wounded.

The Roll of Honour grows as the days pass. Hero follows hero. To give the names of all who have made the supreme sacrifice is impossible; neither can we hope to find fitting words of gratitude and praise.

CONCLUSION

In November, 1916, the famous French aviator, Lieutenant Guynemer, brought down his twenty-first enemy machine, thus establishing a new world's record for aerial warfare. The duel was fought at an altitude of over two miles, after a chase of about forty-four miles, and was of a most dramatic nature.

Suddenly Lieutenant Guynemer, whilst flying many miles behind the German lines, sighted a German squadron of two observation aeroplanes with an escort of two fighting machines heading for the French lines. There was nothing to prevent Lieutenant Guynemer giving immediate battle, except the fact that in the event of being forced to land he would fall within the German lines and be taken prisoner. He therefore took refuge behind some friendly clouds until the German squadron passed ahead of him, and then started the pursuit from behind, closing up sufficiently so that if he should be seen by the German anti-aircraft gunners from below he would be taken for one of the escorting German aeroplanes. For several miles he kept up the pursuit, concealing himself as much as possible from the German machines by keeping behind the clouds.

Then, when the French lines at last appeared below him, he emerged in full view and began the fight. The German machine nearest him chanced to be an observation 'plane, and, darting down on it, he opened his machine-gun fire at an altitude of about 12,000 feet, or just two miles. With unerring aim, he killed the observer with his third bullet, and with the tenth the pilot likewise shot out from the machine, the 'plane at the same time beginning its whirling giddy course down towards the French lines. Although the machine was the second one Guynemer had brought down that day, he at once started after the other three, but they, in the meantime, had all disappeared, having apparently turned back at his very first shot. Without further ado Lieutenant Guynemer started in search of his victims, and succeeded in locating the machine in the ravine of Mocourt.

Amongst British aviators who continue to add to their victories mention must again be made of Flight-Commander Ball, to whose Distinguished Service Order a second bar—the first time such an honour has been conferred—was added in November, 1916. Each passing day brings further evidence of heroic deeds.

On November 29 hostile airships again made a raid over England under the cover of night, but with dire results for the enemy. Two German airships were brought down. An official communication stated that a number of hostile airships approached the north-east coast of England between ten and eleven o'clock. Bombs were dropped on various places in Yorkshire and Durham, but the damage was slight. One airship was attacked by an aeroplane of the Royal Flying Corps and brought down in flames in the sea off the coast of Durham at 11.45 p.m. Another airship crossed into the North Midland Counties and dropped some bombs at various places.

On her return journey she was repeatedly attacked by aeroplanes of the Royal Flying Corps and by guns. She appeared to have been damaged, for the last part of her journey was made at very slow speed, and she was unable to reach the coast before day was breaking. Near the Norfolk coast she apparently succeeded in effecting repairs, and, after passing through gunfire from the land defences, which claim to have made a hit, proceeded east at a high speed, and at an altitude of over 8,000 feet, when she was attacked nine miles out at sea by four machines of the Royal Naval Air Service, while gunfire was opened from an armed trawler. The airship was brought down in flames at 6.45 a.m.

One eye-witness has stated that it was just after daybreak when from the east coast a German airship was seen, travelling slowly from the west. As she passed over the coast the sound of heavy firing was heard, and soon, over a low bank of mist some distance out to sea, a great burst of flame was seen and the stricken raider fell blazing into the sea. A little later a British airman flew in from the sea and descended on the coast. He was given a tremendous ovation. Townspeople carried him shoulder high through streets crowded with cheering people, while sirens of shipping shrieked triumphantly. 'The defence was extraordinarily powerful,' said an official report of the raid issued in Berlin. Such praise from the enemy speaks volumes!

At noon on the following day a German aeroplane managed to reach London and drop bombs. But the fate of this raider also was sealed. On its return journey if fell a victim to our gallant French Allies. Who can now doubt that supremacy in the air is with the *Entente*? Whether in dealing with raiders by night or enemy machines on the western battle-front by day, our heroic allied aviators have proved their superiority.

The names of the heroic naval aviators who brought down the German airship in the manner described are Flight-Sub-Lieutenant E. L. Pulling, Flight-Lieutenant E. Cadbury, and Flight-Lieutenant G. W. R. Fane. The first named officer has been awarded the Distinguished Service Order. His age at the time of his heroic deed was twenty-six years. He was formerly in the Government wireless service, and he received his commission in the Royal Naval Air Service on August 21, 1915. Tireless energy and boundless enthusiasm, combined with great courage, mark him out as an aviator of high promise.

Flight-Lieutenant Egbert Cadbury was twenty-three years of age at the time of receiving the Distinguished Service Cross. At the outbreak of war, he left Trinity College, Cambridge, where he was studying for the law, and joined the *Zarifa* as an A.B., the vessel being a converted yacht manned mostly by Cambridge men. After nearly a year at sea he entered the R.N.A.S., gained his pilot's certificate, and was stationed on the East Coast. He is the youngest son of Mr. George Cadbury.

Flight-Lieutenant Fane joined the Royal Naval Air Service in July, 1915, as a Flight-Sub-Lieutenant. He came straight from Charterhouse and was only nineteen years of age at the time of being decorated. His fellow-airmen speak of him as a pilot of remarkable skill and courage.

In February, 1917, whilst these pages were in proof, it was announced that the first of the officers named above, Flight-Lieutenant E. L. Pulling, D.S.O., had made the 'supreme sacrifice.'

Another body!—Oh, new limbs are ready,
Free, pure, instinct with soul through every nerve.

Ingram Content Group UK Ltd.
Milton Keynes UK
UKHW012100050723
424591UK00001B/72